Modern-Day Xenophobia

Oksana Yakushko

Modern-Day Xenophobia

Critical Historical and Theoretical Perspectives on the Roots of Anti-Immigrant Prejudice

palgrave
macmillan

Oksana Yakushko
Department of Clinical Psychology
Pacifica Graduate Institute
Carpinteria, CA, USA

ISBN 978-3-030-00643-3 ISBN 978-3-030-00644-0 (eBook)
https://doi.org/10.1007/978-3-030-00644-0

Library of Congress Control Number: 2018959242

This Palgrave Macmillan imprint is published by the registered company Springer Nature Switzerland AG
The registered company address is: Gewerbestrasse 11, 6330 Cham, Switzerland

Contents

1 **Introduction** 1
References 7

2 **Hatred of Strangers: Defining Xenophobia and Related Concepts** 11
Xenomania and Xenophilia 12
Xenophobia 12
Xenophobia in Relation to Nativism, Ethnocentrism, Populism, and Extreme Nationalism 14
Xenophobia in Relation to Racism 16
Distinct Signifiers and Outcomes of Xenophobia: Accented Language and Occupational Downgrading 18
Xenophobia in Relation to Anti-semitism 21
Xenophobia in Relation to Islamophobia 22
Xenophobia in Relation to Colonization and Globalization 22
References 23

3 **The Immigrant Tides: Xenophobia in Western History Xenophobia as Neither Universal Nor Historically Invariable** 33
Historical Causes of Human Migrations 34
Historic Xenophobic Treatment of Jews and Other Foreigners in Europe 36

Historical Role of Xenophobia in Enslavement of People 37
Xenophobic Determinants of Unfitness: Social Darwinism and Eugenics in Modern History 38
Recent History of Xenophobia: Fantasizing Immigrant Threats and Fetishizing Immigrants 46
Xenophobic Violence and Brutality 51
References 52

4 Germs, Peacocks, and Scheming Domestics: Theories That Construct or Confront Xenophobia 61
Constructing Xenophobia Through Biologized and Universalized Evolutionary Theories 61
Constructing Xenophobia Through "Realistic" Threat Theories 67
Confronting Xenophobia Through Social Group Theories 68
Confronting Xenophobia Through a Theory of Ethnocentric Guilt 70
Confronting Xenophobia Through Theories of Splitting and Projection 73
Confronting Xenophobia in Relation to Motherland/ Fatherland Discourse 76
Confronting Xenophobia Through Theories the Other and Otherizing 77
Confronting Xenophobia Through Theories of Social Death 79
Confronting Xenophobia Through Theories of Self-Idealization and Psychophobia 80
Confronting Xenophobia Through Post-colonial, De-colonial and Other Critical Theories 81
References 82

5 How to Welcome a Stranger 91
References 95

References 97

Index 123

CHAPTER 1

Introduction

Awareness of xenophobia emerged in recent years because of the rise of anti-immigrant prejudice around the globe. Throughout history relation to foreigners or the newcomers differed based on social, religious, and political factors: at times they were welcomed and even elevated (e.g., xenophilia), at other times they coexisted independently within cultures that seemed to embrace a metropolitan multi-national views (Carballo, Roscoe, & Feinman, 2014; Curtin, 1984; Haynes, 2000). In contrast to these responses, xenophobia reflects a socio-historical mode of an intolerance or hatred of immigrants by the native-born group. Typically, xenophobia is discernable, like prejudices toward other minority groups, through demonizing immigrants as part of an effort to pronounce the host nation-states and their native-born individuals as pure or good while they displace their economic and social problems on the foreign others (Cacho, 2000, 2012; Foner & Fredrickson, 2004; Gabaccia, 2002; Taggart, 2000; Yakushko, 2009b). In addition, because patterns of immigration are determined by critical historical events, such as wars, political instabilities, or other crises, the nation-states directly or indirectly implicated in these conflicts, tend to decry the waves of migration often caused by their own actions (Abromeit, Norman, Marotta, & Chesterton, 2015; Boehnke, Hagan, & Hefler, 1998; Bosma, 2007; Kam & Kinder, 2007; Marsella & Ring, 2003; Sloan, 2005; Williamson, 1997; Zinn, 2010).

O. Yakushko, *Modern-Day Xenophobia*,
https://doi.org/10.1007/978-3-030-00644-0_1

Racism, sexism, homophobia, and other forms of collective prejudice, although focused on distinct human axis of difference, often are the result of shared patterns of social and historical rationales of their exclusion and oppression (Allport, 1954; Baldwin, 1998; Cacho, 2012; Comas-Díaz & Greene, 1994; Fanon, 1959/2008; Foner & Fredrickson, 2004; Gabaccia 2002; McClintock, 1995; Yakushko, 2009b). Racial minorities, women, and anyone perceived as a threat to social order have been demonized by political and religious authorities alike, proclaimed as threats, and blamed for varied national struggles (Fanon, 1959/2008; Patterson, 1982; Ott, 1995; Wistrich, 2011; Zinn, 2010). For example, over the last millennium of Western European history women, Jews, and people living in poverty have been blamed for decline of many nations because of their perceived threat. The *Malleus Maleficarum* or the *Witches Hammer* (Kramer & Sprenger, 1486), a horrific social and scientific manual for identifying and destroying individuals who were perceived as possessed by demonic powers, presented women's sexuality and knowledge as a threat to the survival of Christendom. Similarly, anti-Semitism thrived on the production of cultural artifacts, especially books and tracts that characterized Jews as a menace (Katz, 1980). Eugenics, a scientific movement based on social Darwinism (i.e., human differences explained in terms of survival of the fittest and their procreation), is another example of an effort to identify and eliminate groups considered parasitic to the "civilized" evolutionary fit nations (e.g., racial minorities, people with disabilities, the poor) (Bashford & Levine, 2010; Black, 2003; Selden, 1999; Tucker, 1996; Yakushko, in review). These varied forms of what Wistrich (1999) termed heterophobia or fear and hatred of groups that are perceived as different and as others.

The current rhetoric and policies in relation to immigrants around the globe provides an opportunity to re-examine historical and contemporary patterns specific to anti-immigrant prejudice. In Europe, the United States and many other areas of the world, xenophobia has become a visible and often central socio-cultural ideology that promotes the image of immigrants as dangerous parasitic intruders and immigration as a destructive tidal wave. According to Smithsonian contributor Daley (2016), recent political and social events propelled the term xenophobia into public consciousness because it "summed up the spirit of the age," leading the website Dictionary.com to proclaim xenophobia "2016 word of the year" (online). Daley highlighted that online interest in the term xenophobia was not only stirred by the recent political campaigns in the United States and around the globe, but also by such news as violent attacks on foreigners in South Africa during spring of 2015. Nearly a 1000% increase in searches for xenophobia online was recorded the day following U.K. Brexit vote, Daley reported.

Among the most evident in the now infamous presidential candidacy speech given in June 2015, then-presidential candidate Donald Trump promoted his anti-immigrant policy as a cornerstone of his proposed administration, stating that

> When Mexico sends its people, they're not sending the best. They're sending people that have lots of problems and they're bringing those problems. They're bringing drugs, they're bringing crime. They're rapists and some, I assume, are good people, but I speak to border guards and they're telling us what we're getting. (Silva, 2018, online)

In his attack on sanctuary city policy, specifically in California, Donald Trump proclaimed: "These aren't people. These are animals," further asserting that "California's law provides safe harbor to some of the most vicious and violent offenders on Earth, like MS-13 gang members putting innocent men, women, and children at the mercy of these sadistic criminals" (Korte & Gomez, 2018, online).

These sentiments, while amplified through political and cultural rhetoric, are typical of xenophobic attitudes held by many native-born individuals toward immigrants. The attitudes have direct impact on shaping not only the native-born individuals' opinions but also views that immigrants themselves are made to hold about themselves or other immigrants (Fanon, 1959/2008). In a book of interviews with immigrant women, Berger (2005) highlighted these women's perceptions of discrimination and prejudice as in the story of Tara, a legal immigrant from Central Europe, that described her experiences as being viewed as a "nobody, human dust that can be easily ignored and dismissed" (p. 80).

Xenophobia, like other forms of prejudice, cannot be separated from other forms of social exclusion and violence. Immigrant women have distinct gendered experiences of migration, and often significantly different impacts on their migration status including increased risk of gender violence outside and inside their home, sexual harassment at work, work gender profiling, and tremendous pressures to balance assimilation and adaptation (Berger, 2005; Lemish, 2001; Yakushko & Chronister, 2005; Yakushko & Morgan-Consoli, 2014; Yakushko & Espin, 2010). Immigrant women have the largest earning gap between themselves and almost every other social group (i.e., native-born women, racial minority men); they are also among the most likely group to lack access to health care, education, and legal protections (The Institute for Women's Policy Research, 2018). Xenophobia interacts with sexism and misogyny, often multiplying the effects of these prejudices.

Immigrants of color, especially those from Latin America and Africa, face increased openly racist forms of social violence, including being represented as "animals" or as coming from "shithole countries" (Austin-Hillary, 2018). Racist treatment of immigrants is central to past and present xenophobic rhetoric on immigration, especially in the United States where undesirable immigrant groups were constantly pitted against African Americans (Black, 2003; Foner & Fredrickson, 2004; Kim, 2000; Kuhl, 2002; Lee, 2003; Selden, 1999; Tucker, 1996). Racism, Islamophobia, anti-Semitism, and other forms of prejudice are often directed specifically toward individuals identified as immigrants (Norrasteh, 2016; Taras, 2012; Washington, 2018; Wistrich, 1999).

The intersections of these varied forms of prejudice, like the intersection of multiple forms of human diversity, are receiving increased attention of social scientists and critics (Comas-Diaz & Greene, 1995; Foner & Fredrickson, 2004; Jaynes, 2000; Kam & Kinder, 2007; McClintock, 1995; Merskin, 2011). This volume seeks to contribute to elucidating xenophobia as a specific form of social prejudice and social oppression. History of xenophobia in Western societies, including during the era of the Inquisition-led Witch-Hunts, the Progressive era social Darwinism and eugenics, and the contemporary United States will be used to amplify ways in which xenophobic social attitudes develop and function.

Throughout the book the term immigrant or immigrants is used to denote presence of all foreign born in the country who seek permanent or semi-permanent residence there. Varied terms distinguish between varied types of immigrants: legal immigrants (i.e., in the United States those who have permanent resident status or American citizenship), refugees (i.e., immigrants legally accepted to live in a country as part of an international refugee action or those granted asylum based on specified set of experiences), or undocumented immigrants and migrant workers

(Gabaccia, 2002; Yakushko, 2009b). These categories are overlapping and are determined by political factors such as country's laws, policies, and relations with foreign nations (Akhtar, 2010; LeMay, 2004; Yakushko, 2009b; Yakushko & Blodgett, 2018; Yakushko & Rajan, 2013). For example, individuals from many Central American countries cannot apply for a refugee status based on their experiences of political violence whereas those who arrive from Cuba qualify for such status (U.S. Citizenship & Immigration, 2018; Yakushko & Rajan, 2013). In addition, many immigrants and migrants reside in foreign countries for length of time before returning to their countries of origin. Lastly, debates exist about immigration status or title of those who are forced to migrate, such as through human trafficking for sexual exploitation, labor, or wars, often resulting in complex legal determinations of eligibility (Bales & Soodalter, 2010; Gozdziak & Collett, 2005; U.S. Citizen & Immigration Services, 2018; Yakushko, 2009a).

In this contribution, the term immigrant will apply to all aforementioned categories of individuals who reside permanently or semi-permanently in another country than their country of birth with an intention to establish their personal, family, and professional life in the new country. Moreover, whereas xenophobia is often experienced by immigrant individuals and communities, even if they were in fact born in the host country (i.e., they are not foreign born), an emphasis will be placed on individuals who are not native born and who underwent a process of migration across the borders with the goal of establishing their private and civic identity as being part of a new country. Lastly, many groups of individuals select long sojourns abroad—those engaged in international businesses, religious missionary work, humanitarian endeavors, or international studies—but cannot be considered immigrants because of their primary socio-political identification remains with their country of origin.

Just as with discussion of socially constructed, culturally situated, and politically directed categories of race or gender, immigration and attitudes toward immigrants reflects tremendous complexity and diversity of human experiences and factors (Comas-Diaz & Greene, 1995; Foner & Fredrickson, 2004; Jaynes, 2000; McClintock, 1995). However, just as with considerations of racism and sexism, recognition of an overarching set of prejudicial individual and institutional forms of oppression, considering xenophobia can offer a conceptual lens through which to view anti-immigrant attitudes. Reflecting this complexity, this contribution will review varied definitions of xenophobia and related phenomena, such as nativism, populism, ethnocentrism, racism, anti-Semitism, and Islamophobia. In addition, critical social concepts such as imperialism, colonialism, and globalization will also be noted in relation to perspectives toward immigrants and migration. Brief history of xenophobic periods and movements will be used to highlight trends and origins of particular anti-immigrant periods in Western history. Next I will focus on theories that have been used to explain as well as to justify xenophobic attitudes. Many of these theories will be critiqued in light of emergent perspectives and available demographic data. Alternatively, I will utilize contemporary psychoanalytic, postcolonial, and critical viewpoints to discuss the emergence, the social purpose, and the impact of xenophobia on societies and individuals.

The famous poem, by Emma Lazarus, portion of which is enshrined on the Statue of Liberty in New York City, will serve as a narrative that elucidates views of immigrants and migration. While often noted for its humanitarian impulse, the poem will also serve as an example of how immigrants and immigration are constructed to evoke inhumane and anti-humanitarian reactions to those who seek to migrate.

> ***The New Colossus by Emma Lazarus***
> Not like the brazen giant of Greek fame,
> With conquering limbs astride from land to land;
> Here at our sea-washed, sunset gates shall stand
> A mighty woman with a torch, whose flame
> Is the imprisoned lightning, and her name
> Mother of Exiles. From her beacon-hand
> Glows world-wide welcome; her mild eyes command
> The air-bridged harbor that twin cities frame.
> "Keep, ancient lands, your storied pomp!" cries she
> With silent lips. "Give me your tired, your poor,
> Your huddled masses yearning to breathe free,
> The wretched refuse of your teeming shore.
> Send these, the homeless, tempest-tost to me,
> I lift my lamp beside the golden door!". (Lazarus, 1883, p. 238)

References

Abromeit, J., Norman, Y., Marotta, G., & Chesterton, B. M. (Eds.). (2015). *Transformations of populism in Europe and the Americas: History and recent tendencies*. London: Bloomsbury.

Akhtar, S. (2010). *Immigration and acculturation: Mourning, adaptation, and the next generation*. Lanham, UK: Jason Aronson.

Allport, G. W. (1954). *The nature of prejudice*. Reading, MA: Addison-Wesley.

Austin-Hillery, N. (2018). Trump's racist language serves abusive immigration policies. *Human Rights Campaign Report*. Retrieved November 1, 2018, from https://www.hrw.org/news/2018/05/22/trumps-racistlanguage-serves-abusive-immigration-policies.

Baldwin, J. (1998). *Collected essays*. New York: Library of America.

Bales, K., & Soodalter, R. (2010). *The slave next door: Human trafficking and slavery in America today*. Berkeley, CA: University of California Press.

Bashford, A., & Levine, P. (Eds.). (2010). *The Oxford handbook of the history of eugenics*. New York: Oxford University Press.

Berger, R. (2005). *Immigrant women tell their stories*. New York: The Haworth Press.

Black, E. (2003). *War against the weak: Eugenics and America's campaign to create a master race*. New York, NY: Four Walls Eight Windows.

Boehnke, K., Hagan, J., & Hefler, G. (1998). On the development of xenophobia in Germany: The adolescent years. *Journal of Social Issues, 54*, 585–603.

Bosma, U. (2007). Beyond the Atlantic: Connecting migration and world history in the age of imperialism, 1840–1940. *International Review of Social History, 52*(1), 116–123.

Cacho, L. M. (2000). 'The people of California are suffering': The ideology of white injury in discourses of immigration. *Journal for Cultural Research, 4*(4), 389–418.

Cacho, L. M. (2012). *Social death: Racialized rightlessness and the criminalization of the unprotected*. New York, NY: New York University Press.

Carballo, D. M., Roscoe, P., & Feinman, G. M. (2014). Cooperation and collective action in the cultural evolution of complex societies. *Journal of Archaeological Method and Theory, 21*(1), 98–133.

Comas-Díaz, L., & Greene, B. (Eds.). (1994). *Women of color: Integrating ethnic and gender identities in psychotherapy*. New York: Guilford.

Comas-Diaz, L., & Greene, B. (1995). *Women of color*. New York: Guilford.

Curtin, P. (1984). *Cross-cultural trade in world history*. Cambridge: Cambridge University Press.

Daley, J. (2016, November 29). Why xenophobia is Dictionary.com word of the year. *Smithsonian Smart News*. Retrieved from https://www.smithsonianmag.com/smart-news/why-xenophobia-dictionarycoms-word-year-180961225/.

Fanon, F. (1959/2008). *Black skin/White masks*. New York: Grove Press.
Foner, N., & Fredrickson, G. M. (Eds.). (2004). *Not just Black and White: Historical and contemporary perspectives on immigration, race, and ethnicity in the United States*. New York: Russell Sage.
Gabaccia, D. R. (2002). *Immigration and American diversity: A concise introduction*. Malden, MA: Blackwell.
Gozdziak, E. M., & Collett, E. A. (2005). Research on human trafficking in North America: A review of literature. *International Migration, 43*(1–2), 99–128.
Haynes, S. (2000). *Etruscan civilization: A cultural history*. Los Angeles, CA: Getty Publications.
Jaynes, G. D. (Ed.). (2000). *Immigration and race: New challenges for American democracy*. New Haven, CT: Yale University Press.
Kam, C. D., & Kinder, D. R. (2007). Terror and ethnocentrism: Foundations of American support for the war on terrorism. *The Journal of Politics, 69*(2), 320–338.
Katz, J. (1980). *From prejudice to destruction: Anti-semitism, 1700–1933*. Cambridge: Harvard University Press.
Kim, C. J. (2000). *Bitter fruit: The politics of Black-Korean conflict in New York City*. New Haven, CT: Yale University Press.
Korte, G., & Gomez, A. (2018, May 16). Trump ramps up rhetoric on undocumented immigrants: 'These aren't people. These are animals'. *The USA Today*. Retrieved from https://www.usatoday.com/story/news/politics/2018/05/16/trump-immigrants-animals-mexico-democrats-sanctuary-cities/617252002/.
Kramer, H., & Sprenger, J. (1486). *The Malleus Maleficarum of Heinrich Kramer and James Sprenger* (W. Lovelace & C. Rice, Trans. [1928/1948]).
Kuhl, S. (2002). *The Nazi connection: Eugenics, American racism, and German national socialism*. New York: Oxford University Press.
Lazarus, E. (1883). The new colossus. *A Century of Immigration, 1820–1924*. Library of Congress. Retrieved from https://memory.loc.gov/ammem/awhhtml/awlaw3/immigration.html.
Lee, R. G. (2003). *Orientals: Asian American in popular culture*. Philadelphia, PA: Temple University Press.
LeMay, M. C. (2004). *U.S. immigration: A reference handbook*. Santa Barbara, CA: ABC CLIO.
Lemish, D. (2001). The whore and the other: Israeli images of female immigrants from the former USSR. *Gender & Society, 14*, 333–349.
Marsella, A. J., & Ring, E. (2003). Human migration and immigration: An overview. In L. L. Adler & U. P. Gielen (Eds.), *Migration: Immigration and emigration in international perspective* (pp. 3–22). Westport, CT: Praeger.
McClintock, A. (1995). *Imperial leather: Race, gender and sexuality in the colonial contest*. New York: Routledge.

Merskin, D. L. (2011). *Media, minorities, and meaning: A critical introduction.* New York: Peter Lang.
Norrasteh, A. (2016). *Terrorism and immigration: Risk analysis.* The CATO Institute, Policy Analysis No. 798. Retrieved June 18, 2018, from https://www.cato.org/publications/policy-analysis/terrorism-immigration-risk-analysis.
Ott, E. M. (1995). Effects of the male female ration at work: Policewomen and male nurses. *Psychology of Women Quarterly, 13,* 41–57.
Patterson, O. (1982). *Slavery and social death.* Cambridge, MA: Harvard University Press.
Selden, S. (1999). *Inheriting shame: The story of eugenics and racism in America.* New York: Teachers College Press.
Silva, C. (2018). Trump's full list of 'racist' comments about immigrants, Muslims and others. *The Newsweek.* Retrieved from https://www.newsweek.com/trumps-full-list-racist-comments-about-immigrants-muslims-and-others-779061.
Sloan, T. (2005). Globalization, poverty, and social justice. In G. Nelson & I. Prilleltensky (Eds.), *Community psychology: In pursuit of liberation and well-being* (pp. 309–329). New York: Palgrave.
Taggart, P. (2000). *Populism.* Buckingham: Open University Press.
Taras, R. (2012). *Xenophobia and Islamophobia in Europe.* Edinburgh, UK: Edinburgh University Press.
The Institute for Women's Policy Research. (2018). *Immigrant women.* Retrieved June 19, 2018, from https://statusofwomendata.org/immigrant-women/.
Tucker, W. H. (1996). *The science and politics of racial research.* Urbana-Champaign: University of Illinois Press.
U.S. Citizen & Immigration Services. (2018). *Green Card eligibility categories.* https://www.uscis.gov/greencard/eligibility-categories.
Washington, J. (2018, June 27). Here is just some of the hateful abuse immigrants face in detention centers. *The Nation.* Retrieved June 19, 2018, from https://www.thenation.com/article/just-hateful-abuse-immigrants-face-detention-centers/.
Williamson, J. (1997). Globalization and inequality, past and present. *The World Bank Research Observer, 12,* 117–135.
Wistrich, R. S. (1999). The devil, the Jews and hatred of the "other." In R. S. Wistrich (Ed.), *Demonizing the other.* Amsterdam, NL: Harwood Academic.
Wistrich, R. S. (2011). *Demonizing the other: Antisemitism, racism and xenophobia.* London, UK: Routledge.
Yakushko, O. (2009a). Human trafficking: A review for mental health professionals. *International Journal for the Advancement of Counselling, 31*, 158–167. https://doi.org/10.1007/s10447-009-9075-3.

Yakushko, O. (2009b). Xenophobia: Understanding the roots and consequences of negative attitudes towards immigrants. *The Counseling Psychologist, 37*, 36–66.

Yakushko, O. (In review). The evolution of eugenics in U.S. Psychology: On a disciplinary promotion of the "science of race betterment".

Yakushko, O., & Blodgett, E. (2018). Counseling recent immigrants. In CC. Lee (Ed.), *Multicultural issues in counseling: New approaches to diversity* (pp. 215–227). Alexandria, VA: American Counseling Association.

Yakushko, O., & Chronister, K. (2005). Immigrant women and counseling: The invisible Others. *Journal of Counseling and Development, 83*, 292–299.

Yakushko, O., & Espín, O. (2010). Immigrant and refugee women. In H. Landrine & N. F. Russo (Eds.), *Handbook of diversity in feminist psychology* (pp. 535–558). Washington, DC: American Psychological Association.

Yakushko, O., & Morgan-Consoli, M. L. (2014). Gendered stories of adaptation and resistance: A feminist multiple case study of immigrant women. *International Journal for the Advancement of Counselling, 36*(1), 70–83.

Yakushko, O., & Rajan, I. (2013). Refugees. In *The multicultural psychology case studies.* Thousand Oaks, CA: Sage (with student).

Zinn, H. (2010). *The twentieth century: A people's history.* New York: Harper & Row.

CHAPTER 2

Hatred of Strangers: Defining Xenophobia and Related Concepts

Abstract Xenophobia as well as related ideas have been defined and constructed in varied ways in Western scholarship. This chapter reviews definitions of pro-foreigner concepts such as xenophilia and concepts associated to with anti-immigrants prejudice such as ethnocentrism, anti-Semitism, nativism, and Islamophobia. In addition, discussions of colonialism and globalization help expound theoretical perspectives on xenophobia.

Keywords Xenophobia · Xenophilia · Anti-immigrant prejudice · Ethnocentrism · Nativism

According to a historical review by the Merriam-Webster (2018) of the use term xenophobia in English language is recent in comparison to other terms related to prejudice. Based on its definition of xenophobia as "fear or hatred of strangers of foreigners," the earliest citation appears to in London's *The Daily News* in April of 1880, claiming that such fear and hatred of foreigners is "always unintelligent." Another term noted by Merriam-Webster in English language use prior to nineteenth century that denoted anti-immigrant attitudes was misoxenie, a word used to describe a person who displayed hatred of strangers. Despite this lack of clear terms, it appears that prejudice toward foreigners, strangers, and immigrants has been part of histories of many modern nation-states (Ana, 1999; Perea, 1997).

O. Yakushko, *Modern-Day Xenophobia*,
https://doi.org/10.1007/978-3-030-00644-0_2

Xenomania and Xenophilia

It is important to note that blanket dislike of individuals and artifacts deemed foreign is neither universal nor constant in cultures. Admiration, partiality toward and even veneration of things considered foreign or different have also been noted, including fetishizing or idolizing particular groups and their cultures. Merriam-Webster (2018) analysis found that the term xenophobia was originally used to oppose xenomania, defined as "an ordinate attachment to foreign things" (online), which was claimed to be more problematic than dislike or fear of strangers. More recently, the term xenophilia has been used to describe a tendency in organisms (animals and plants) toward the preference for influences outside their own species as well as among individuals and groups who may perceive their own culture as inferior to another culture, such as ancient Romans' view of Greeks were superior to them (Burke, 2005). Recently, Stürmer and colleagues (2013) used the term xenophilia to denote favorable attitudes toward immigrants, other cultures, and indigenous groups whereas Friedman (2009) utilized the term more negatively to denote a type of romanticism that privileged non-dominant non-Western religious traditions without attending to their potentially controversial treatment of human experiences.

Xenophobia

Nevertheless, despite these rare emphases on favoring foreign groups, practices and ideas, xenophobia as a form of anti-immigrant prejudice remains far more prevalent as a contemporary social concept. Similarly, although terms such as Afrophilia, allophilia, and allosemitism are ostensibly views that represent opposites to anti-Black racism, heterophobia, and anti-Semitism, their contemporary use is limited. In addition, fetishizing of other cultures have been highlighted as another form of social oppression, either as the evidence of internalized inferiority that resulted from history of colonization such as the "Mongrel complex" among the Latin Americans when they compare themselves unfavorably to White Europeans (Young, 2005) or as varied forms of racial fetishisms and cultural appropriations common among the privileged Western individuals (Ahmed, 2013; Bhabha, 1983; McClintock, 1995; Zizek, 1997).

Thus, the most commonly agreed term that denotes anti-immigrant prejudice is xenophobia. According to Boehnke's (2001) definition provided at the International Migration, Racism, Discrimination, and Xenophobia Conference held by multiple international human rights groups under the United Nations auspices, xenophobia is "an attitudinal orientation of hostility against non-natives in a given population" (online). The Merriam-Webster dictionary's (2018) definition of xenophobia as the "fear and hatred of strangers or foreigners or of anything that is strange or foreign" highlights that the term has been historically used to emphasize a sense of fright of the outsiders (online).

Other definitions of xenophobia emphasize similar sets of fearful or hostile attitudes toward foreigners. Reynolds and Vine (1987) stated that xenophobia is a "psychological state of hostility or fear towards outsiders" (p. 28). Crowther (1995) stressed that xenophobia focuses on individuals who come from "other countries," and toward whom the native individuals have "an intense dislike or fear" (p. 1385).

The United National reports on xenophobia around the globe often highlight varied and related definitions of xenophobia. For example, in its report on xenophobia in South Africa, produced for the United Nations Refugee Agency by Misago, Freemantle, and Landau (2015), proposed a

> holistic definition of xenophobia as, "attitudes, prejudices and behaviour that reject, exclude and often vilify persons based on the perception that they are outsiders or foreigners to the community, society or national identity."... Importantly, this definition includes both negative attitudes and chauvinistic behavior [which] translates into a broad spectrum of behaviors including discriminatory, stereotyping and dehumanizing remarks; discriminatory policies and practices by government and private officials such as exclusion from public services to which target groups are entitled; selective enforcement of by-laws by local authorities; assault and harassment by state agents particularly the police and immigration officials; as well as public threats and violence commonly known as xenophobic violence that often results in massive loss of lives and livelihoods. (online)

This expanded definition also highlights the varied expressions of anti-immigrant prejudice that underline its similarity to other forms of social violence such as racism, which include not only policies and practices but also expressed emotional and cognitive evaluations of immigrants by the native-born individuals. In my work on xenophobia as a social psychological construct, I defined xenophobia as "a form of attitudinal, affective, and behavioral prejudice toward immigrants and those perceived as foreign" (Yakushko, 2009b, p. 72).

Undoubtedly, xenophobia, like other forms of social prejudice, overlaps with other concepts used to define and describe social attitudes. Anti-immigrant prejudice is routinely described in relation to perceived economic, cultural, religious, political or social motivations (American Immigration Council, 2013; Chavez, 2001; Dodson, 2010; Esses, Dovidio, Jackson, & Armstrong, 2001; Esses, Dovidio, Semenya, & Jackson, 2005; Florack, Bless, & Piontkowski, 2003; Fry, 2001; Lee, Martinez, & Rosenfeld, 2001; Misago et al., 2015; Yakushko, 2009b). Despite some shared cultural frameworks that seem to produce or incite xenophobia, its manifestation typically focus on specific time- and culture-bound aspects of hatred toward immigrants such as the Chinese in the early twentieth century United States or North African refugees in twenty-first century Europe (Art, 2011; Perea, 1997). These instances of xenophobia emphasize differential foci on language as well as cultural or religious practices that are typically represented as dangerous to the native-born communities. Moreover, xenophobic attitudes and practices are likely to be based on as well as become amplified by existing prejudices endemic in a particular culture such as those based on skin color or on religious affiliation (UNHCR, 2001; Yakushko & Blodgett, 2018; Yakushko & Morgan-Consoli, 2012).

Xenophobia in Relation to Nativism, Ethnocentrism, Populism, and Extreme Nationalism

Thus, alternate concepts and terms help elucidate xenophobia as a category of human prejudice. Among these concepts are nativism, ethnocentrism, populism, extreme nationalism. According to Higham (1988) nativism is

> an intense opposition to an internal minority on the grounds of its foreign (i.e., "un-American") connections. Specific nativist antagonisms may and do, vary widely in response to the changing character of minority irritants and the shifting conditions of the day; but through each separate hostility runs the connecting, energizing force of modern nationalism. While drawing on much broader cultural antipathies and ethnocentric judgments, nativism translates them into zeal to destroy the enemies of a distinctively American way of life. (p. 2)

Guia (2016) further emphasized that nativism is characterized by an emphasis on differentiating those who are native-born versus those who were born outside the national borders, thus providing mechanisms for a specific form of social construction in modern states along the axis of the birthplace (i.e., differentiating access to political rights and representation) with the primary goal of restricting "immigration in order to maintain some deemed essential characteristics of a given political unit" (p. v). Recent forms of nativism often overlap with nationalism and populism when it takes form of juxtaposition between "the people" (i.e., "us") and "the foreigners" (i.e., "not us") (Abromeit, Marotta, Chesterton, & Norman, 2015; Gellner, 1995; Fritzsche, 1994; Schirmer, 1998; Taggart, 2000).

Prior to recent rise in an interest in xenophobia, nativism appeared to be a far more common term in discussing anti- or pro-immigrant attitudes and policies. Nativism and populism at times have been presented as expected concepts (i.e., national pride or preference for one's own national group) in contrast to xenophobia, which denotes a form of social prejudice and oppression (Fry, 2001; Gellner, 1995; Perea, 1997). For example, Guia (2016) discussed that nativism can occur across the political and attitudinal social spectrums, both on the so-called right and the left, whereas xenophobia is perceived to be a broader concept that specifically denotes negative valuation and treatment of immigrants.

However, in historical accounts such demarcations of left and right-wing ideologies in relation to immigrants are far more blurred. For example, many eugenicists in Europe and the United States who considered themselves to be progressive and liberal (e.g., Karl Pearson, George B. Shaw, Margaret Sanger, Thomas Roosevelt), promoted utopian ideas of developing Western nations through "science" of Darwinist evolutionary theories into the Master races by either closing borders to all the evolutionary unfit (i.e., non-Nordic or non-Aryan) immigrants or controlling these immigrants' procreation by sterilizing them (Bashford & Levine, 2010; Selden, 1999; Yakushko & Blodgett, 2018). In fact, contemporary justifications of eugenics and social Darwinism, offered by evolutionary psychology and behavioral genetics scientists, emphasize that such eugenic policies are acceptable because they have been supported by progressive and liberal (rather than only right-wing Nazi) thinkers (Lynn, 2001; Pinker, 2002, 2018). Focus on controlling immigration, as supposedly a form of environmental stewardship, by emphasizing the Malthusian "overpopulation" threat, is also common among those who view themselves as environmentalists (Connelly, 2006; Ervin, 1994; Solnit, 2004; Tactaquin, 1998). Thus, xenophobia, just as other forms of prejudice, is not the exclusive domain of far-right and politically conservative individuals and groups but can be found in varied forms and with varied rationalizations across the spectrums of political, social, racial-ethnic, and other human differences.

The notion of ethnocentrism offers another related conceptual explanatory framework in regard to attitudes toward foreign-born individuals and groups (Brewer & Campbell, 1976; Cashdan, 2001; LeVine & Campbell, 1972). Ethnocentrism typically focuses on evaluation of other cultural groups based on the standards of one's own group, marked by devaluation of behaviors, social customs, religious practices, and language that are perceived as belonging to those perceived as the outside group (Brewer & Campbell, 1976). According to Kam & Kinder (2007), "Ethnocentrism is a general outlook on groups and group relations, one that partitions the social world into us and them, into friend and foe," which typically relies on stereotypes and categorizations, which privilege the in-group while depreciating the out-group (p. 323).

Xenophobia in Relation to Racism

Among the most closely related and often interchangeably used with xenophobia concepts is racism. The term race in its original formulation by the European scholars focused specifically on national origins that perceived racial and ethnic minorities, whether foreign-born or native-born, as belonging in origin to other national locations (Alexander, 1987; Bobo, 1988; Fernando, 1993; Merskin, 2011; Miles, 1982; Navas, 1998; Schirmer, 1998; Selden, 1999; Silva, 2003; Watts, 1996). Among the most influential theorists to reify the notion of racial differences as universal and biological facts was Charles Darwin (1859) who in his *The Origins of the Species: Or, The Preservation of Favoured Races in the Struggle for Life* stated that the "grade of civilization… seems a most important element in the success of nations" (p. 239) while promoting his concepts that survival of the fittest "races" (i.e., species) of both animals and humans was evident in their supposed evolutionary status. Darwin (1859, 1888) routinely compared the native-born "English" with foreign-born "races," specifically Jews, while his followers and eugenicists such as Galton (1869, 1904) and Pearson (1905, 1911) produced scientific studies on the parasitic effects of foreign-born migration from the "lower races" on British society. Thus, the intersections of historical and contemporary forms of racism and xenophobia continually appear in Western social history, especially through the use of scientific rationalizations of prejudice and oppressive policies (Fanon, 1959; Smith, 1985; Selden, 1999; Tucker, 1996).

When the primary social differentiation between the native and non-native-born individuals focuses on the supposed racial differences, xenophobia and racism indeed function in indistinguishable and mutually reinforcing manner (Cacho, 2012; Fernando, 1993; Miles, 1982; Wimmer, 1997; Yakushko, 2009b, 2010a). In the subsequent chapter on history of Western xenophobia, I will discuss how anti-immigrant prejudices were shaped by racist ideologies as well as how racism drew on derogatory attitudes toward immigrants. Certainly, in the United States and other Western countries many racial minority groups, even if they are native-born, are presented perpetually as immigrants (Bhabha, 1994; Lee, 2003; Moradi & Hasan, 2004; Sue, 2003). Upon arrival to racially stratified societies like the United States and Europe, immigrants are placed into specific racial categories that denote their social standing and treatment (Fernando, 1993; Jasinskaja-Lahti, Liebkind, & Perhoniemi, 2006; Silva, 2003; UNHCR, 2001; Wimmer, 1997; Yakushko, 2009b). Immigrants who are perceived as racially similar to the native-born majority may receive preferential treatment though still being treated as inferior to native-born (Foner & Fredrickson, 2004; Jaynes, 2000) whereas those who are identified as visibly different based on skin color are likely to experience significant racialized forms of social violence and exclusion, amplified by their status as foreign-born (Cacho, 2012; Jasinskaja-Lahti et al., 2006; Jaynes, 2000).

On the other hand, it is important to distinguish xenophobia and racism. Racism typically reflects prejudice based on socially constructed notions related to visible phenotypical markers, such as skin color, as well as biological markers such as supposed racial differences in genetic make-up or brain size (Castles & Miller, 1993; Helms, 1994; Helms & Talleyrand, 1997; Marger, 1997; Rushton, 1995). In contrast, xenophobic views focus on the status of an individual as being foreign-born, notwithstanding of their visible difference or similarity with the native-born individuals (Boehnke, Hagan, & Hefler, 1998; Hannaford, 1996; Wimmer, 1997; Yakushko, 2009b). Undoubtedly, because of European colonization, slavery, and subsequent scientific racism (e.g., social Darwinism, eugenics), the superiority of White or light skinned individuals over Black, Brown or darker-skinned individuals transcends national ethnocultural boundaries and shapes views toward immigrants as well (Gabbacia, 2002; Helms & Talleyrand, 1997). Many immigrants to Western cultures face racism in addition to xenophobia because of their visible racial differences although xenophobia often takes distinct and additional forms of discrimination in their lives (Bebout, 2016; Bolaffi, 2003; Cacho, 2012; Espenshade, 2000; Fernando, 1993; Foner & Fredrickson, 2004; Wimmer, 1997). However, racial differences may not be central to mistreatment of immigrants whose foreign-born status, their foreign cultural or religious practices as well as their accented language can serve as signifiers of inferiority for the dominant group (Berger, 2005; Hansen, Rakić, & Steffens, 2017; Taras, 2012; Yakushko, 2009b). Indeed, prejudice and violence toward foreign-born occurs in communities without any notable racial differences between the native-born and immigrant individuals (Lemish, 2001; Misago et al., 2015; Pedahzur & Yishai, 1999).

Distinct Signifiers and Outcomes of Xenophobia: Accented Language and Occupational Downgrading

One of the frequent signifiers (i.e., perceived shared characteristics that evoke reactions) is linguistic ability to speak the language of the host country and to speak it without an accent (Yakushko, 2010a, 2010b). In the United States one of the only accents that receives a privileged treatment is U.K. English, which Jones (2001) connected to colonial, imperialist, and racialized perception of what constitutes a good immigrant to the United States (i.e., intelligence and adaptation as measured by capacity to speak English). Rigid focus on English language production or English-Only policies often reflect xenophobic rhetoric and policies in the United States (Wolfram & Schilling-Estes, 2006). Services to reduce immigrant accent through English language courses, even if an immigrant is proficient in the language, are openly offered as a form of supposed bias reduction by the native-born individuals toward the foreigners (Hernandez, 1993). Studies have shown that despite considerable evidence of immigrants' prior education and accomplishments, their capacity to speak without an accent is often used to make explicit and implicit judgments about their intelligence

(Bresnahan, Ohashi, Nebashi, Liu, & Shearman, 2002; Edwards, 1999; Gluszek & Dovidio, 2010). Discrimination against immigrants is justified specifically because of accented English is used as a stereotyped (prejudicial) proxy not just for individuals' capacities but also their credibility, integrity, and trustworthiness (Hosoda, & Stone-Romero, 2010; Lev-Ari & Keysar, 2010).

Although prejudice toward distinct patterns of English about native-born Americans can also serve as such a signifier that evokes prejudice (Sue, 2003), accented English or limited English language (or other native languages in case of immigrants in Europe, Asia, and Africa) capacities often evoke blatant forms of xenophobic prejudice regardless of immigrant's racial or even cultural similarity with the native-born group (Ng, 2007; Rakić, Steffens, & Mummendey, 2011). Around the world immigrants' accented language often serves to legitimize discrimination, including in employment, education, financial services, and health care (de Souza, Pereira, Camino, de Lima, & Torres, 2016). In fact, in experimental studies a foreign-born looking individual who has a native-born accent loses their perceived competence and skills as soon as their accent increases: they are perceived "more competent when seen rather than heard" (Hansen et al., 2017, title).

Specifically, occupational downgrading is among the most common visible signs of xenophobic treatment of immigrants, which often disregards their actual levels of education, skill, and capacity, which may or may not be mitigated after a long period of immigrants' residence in their new country (Akresh, 2008). Most Western nations have policies that encourage immigration of highly skilled workers and exceptionally talented individuals, often referred to as the "brain drain" (Gabbacia, 2002; Yakushko, 2009b). However, majority of scholars note that these immigrants invariably experienced occupational downgrading, deskilling, and blatant discrimination in contrast to native-born workers with the same set of skills (Creese & Wiebe, 2012; Dean & Wilson, 2009; Pratt, 1999; Remennick, 2005). Bauder (2003) termed this treatment the "brain abuse" (p. 699).

As noted earlier, in the United States foreign-born, especially foreign-born women, have the largest earning gap of all the groups (Larsen, 2004; Lin & Green, 2001; Pratt, 1999; Remennick, 2005; The Institute for Women's Policy Research, 2018). In addition, even with accumulation of skills and experiences over time, immigrants do not receive the same "returns" (i.e., salary increases, benefits) as native-born individuals employed in the same occupations positions (Eckstein & Weiss, 2004). Moreover, because immigrants are often tracked into occupations where it is difficult or impossible to receive promotion or job upgrading, such opportunities may be limited (Pew Hispanic Center, 2016). Immigrants' own perceptions that they are undeserving of advancements, based on internalizing that their standing in society as lower, may also contribute to this pattern (Segura, 1989).

Another common promoted stereotype is that most of the immigrants seek to start small ethnic businesses (Waldinger, Ward, & Aldrich, 1985). These ethnic businesses are in fact frequently promoted as "model" immigrant social behavior, contrasting supposedly hard-working and enterprising immigrants (especially those from Asia) to native-born minority individuals, who are stereotyped as lazy and unenterprising (especially African Americans) (Espenshade, 2000; Kim, 2000; Merskin, 2011; Thornton & Mizuno, 1999; Waldinger, 1997). These intentional efforts present immigrants as a threat to native-born minorities and misdirect attention from the actual sources of oppression (Yakushko, 2009b). Notably, the immigrant-run ethnic small businesses may be another intentional myth because these enterprises are neither common nor successful, considering that in Western cultures large corporations dominate all areas of economy, having nearly erased existence of so-called small business operations with few exceptions (Waldinger et al., 1985). However, even if promotion of anti-immigrant attitudes among native-born minorities is a culturally motivated strategy, xenophobic treatment of immigrants by native-born marginalized groups has been damaging, such as African-Americans' negative actions toward Black immigrants and Asian immigrants or native-born Latinos' toward newly arriving Latinos (Hovey, Rojas, Kain, & Magaña, 2000; Kim, 2000; Morrison, 1994; Ochoa, 2000).

Thus, xenophobia most typically reflects nativist and ethnocentric attitudes that define difference vis-a-vie place of birth or the national origin, which is perceived as inferior to the native-born status (Hagendoorn & Sniderman, 2001). Even ethnic similarity and histories of shared oppression do not appear to mitigate xenophobia in many cases, such as in Israel where Israeli Jews display significant xenophobic attitudes toward Jewish immigrants from the former USSR (Pedahzur & Yishai, 1999; Remennick, 2005; Shamai & Ilatov, 2001). Lastly, as noted above, xenophobic prejudices are often purposefully stirred among the native-born racial minority individuals, often in an effort to present the foreign-born, rather than the privileged majority individuals, as supposed rivals for limited resources (Espanshade, 2000; Kim, 2000; Morrison, 1994; Thornton & Mizuno, 1999; Waldinger, 1997).

Xenophobia in Relation to Anti-semitism

A form of historical and current racism that helps further elucidate this difference is anti-Semitism. In fact, the term "race" as a scientific concept of institutionalized and cultural racial difference was used by Hirschfeld in 1930 in relation to Jews (Merskin, 2011). Social Darwinists (i.e., applying observations on animals in regard to survival of the fittest and procreative competition to human behavior), including Charles Darwin (1859, 1888, 1898) himself and eugenicists (Galton, 1869; Pearson, 1905) used the term "race" specifically to refer to Jews and other "uncivilized" and "primitive" national groups in their voluminous scientific anti-Semitic and racist scholarship. Historical and current anti-Semitism represented Jews as foreigners, since the invasion of Israel and displacement of Jewish people by Romans and later Christianization of Europe (Wistrich, 2011).

Throughout recent history Jewish presence has been routinely presented as alien and dangerous, culminating in modern anti-Semitism that developed over the past two centuries. Not only diasporic Jews were viewed as a threat to Western societies, but also their movement across borders were seen as especially problematic and often represented as one country's problematic "refuse" which must be stopped and rejected by the host country (Wistrich, 2011). The eugenic United States scholars such as Stanley G. Hall (1881), the founder of American academic psychology and the first president of the American Psychological Association, who was a eugenicist and social Darwinist, decried the destruction of Western cultures by "rapacious Jews" who were continually represented as dangerous foreign intruders (p. 236). Steiner (1909), who characterized himself as an Americanized Jew who converted to Christianity, in his eugenic xenophobic work entitled *The Immigrant Tide*, warned against the parasitic racial effects of immigrant Jews seeking entrance to the United States because of their supposed tendencies to be criminal, avaricious, sexually amoral, non-religious, over-populating, and politically disloyal. Thus, history of anti-Semitism is often marked by focus on Jews as foreigners and immigrants, even if they were native-born, often tracing their roots to the same location through many generations.

Xenophobia in Relation to Islamophobia

More recent form of prejudice that is related to xenophobia is Islamophobia. Although religious prejudice toward the Muslims in Europe, as evidenced by the Crusades, is long-standing, the more recent political wrangling has resulted in an increased prejudice toward individuals who are perceived as Muslim (Taras, 2012). Taras defined Islamophobia as unfounded antagonistic prejudice and discrimination toward both the religion of Islam and individuals who either are practicing Muslims or who are perceived as such. Individuals who practice Islam in context of non-Islamic states, regardless of their racial or national affiliation, are typically represented as threatening foreigners, whether they are indeed immigrant or not (Poole & Richardson, 2010).

Xenophobia in Relation to Colonization and Globalization

In addition to these concepts, critical social scientists emphasize other concepts that help elucidate the nature and function of xenophobia. Bhabha (1990), a critical postcolonial scholar, highlighted that the concept of nation-states is historically recent since both Western and non-Western societies have been organized around alternative entities such as large multi-state empires, small kingdoms or fiefdoms as well as individual tribes, cities, and villages. Paradoxically, imperialism and colonization were among the driving sources of creating firm boundaries between native-born individuals (i.e., British, Spanish) and the foreign-born natives (i.e., indigenous groups, other immigrant groups), even though the colonizers were themselves immigrants or foreigners (Ashcroft, 2013; Bhabha, 1994, 1995; Lorenz & Watkins, 2001; Zinn, 2010). Similarly, globalization, which emphasizes worldwide convergence of economic, social, and cultural influences, has been comparably implicated in the increased rigidity of boundaries between native-born and foreign-born individuals while enabling human migration because of global inequalities as well as cross-national environmental and political crises (Ashcroft, 2013; Sloan, 2005). In addi tion, cultural globalization promotes ideologies that elevate Western societies as idealized locations for living (i.e., Hollywoodized view of the United States) while simultaneously barring entrance or punishing newcomers seeking a place in these exalted locations because they represent as a threat to perfected social visions (McClintock, 1995; Memmi, 2013; Merskin, 2011; Perea, 1997; Selden, 1999; Yakushko & Blodgett, 2018).

This review of xenophobia and related concepts points to a complex, interlocking and inter-related network of socio-cultural norms, all of which are grounded in historical influences. The absence of historical accounts that offer critical and non-dominant perspectives results in perpetuation of prejudice and social violence (Baldwin, 1965; Fanon, 1959; Zinn, 2010). Historical accounts of foreign others from non-privileged backgrounds (i.e., foreign-born poor) has often presented them as dangerous, parasitic, inhuman, and villainous whereas socially powerful immigrants who colonized other countries through military, cultural, or political efforts have always characterized themselves as salvific and progressive additions to new lands (Merskin, 2011; Yakushko & Blodgett, 2018; Zinn, 2010). History of xenophobia or prejudice toward foreigners will focus specifically on systematic demonization and exclusion of foreigners who sought to migrate by the dominant native-born social groups.

References

Abromeit, J., Marotta, G., Chesterton, B. M., & Norman, Y. (Eds.). (2015). *Transformations of populism in Europe and the Americas: History and recent tendencies*. London: Bloomsbury.

Ahmed, S. (2013). *Strange encounters: Embodied others in post-coloniality*. London: Routledge.

Akresh, I. R. (2008). Occupational trajectories of legal US immigrants: Downgrading and recovery. *Population and Development Review, 34*(3), 435–456.

Alexander, P. (1987). *Racism, resistance, and revolution*. London: Bookmarks.

American Immigration Council. (2013). *The economic blame game: Immigration and unemployment*. Washington, DC: Immigration Policy Center. Retrieved on June 2018, from https://www.americanimmigrationcouncil.org/sites/default/files/research/economic_blame_game.pdf.

Ana, O. S. (1999). 'Like an animal I was treated': Anti-immigrant metaphor in US public discourse. *Discourse and Society, 10*(2), 191–224.
Art, D. (2011). *Inside the radical right: The development of anti-immigrant parties in Western Europe*. Cambridge, UK: Cambridge University Press.
Ashcroft, B. (2013). *Post-colonial transformation*. London: Routledge.
Baldwin, J. (1965). White man's guilt. *Ebony Magazine*, 47–48.
Bashford, A., & Levine, P. (Eds.). (2010). *The Oxford handbook of the history of eugenics*. New York: Oxford University Press.
Bauder, H. (2003). "Brain abuse", or the devaluation of immigrant labour in Canada. *Antipode, 35*(4), 699–717.
Bebout, L. (2016). *Whiteness on the border: Mapping the U.S. racial imagination in Brown and White*. New York: New York University Press.
Berger, R. (2005). *Immigrant women tell their stories*. New York: The Haworth Press.
Bhabha, H. (1990). *DissemiNation: Time, narrative, and the margins of the modern nation*. London: Routledge.
Bhabha, H. K. (1983). The other question: Difference, discrimination and the discourses of colonialism. *Screen, 24*(6), 18–36. https://doi.org/10.1093/screen/24.6.18.
Bhabha, H. K. (1994). *The location of culture*. London: Routledge.
Bhabha, H. K. (1995). *Nation and narration*. London: Routledge.
Bobo, L. (1988). Group conflict, prejudice, and the paradox of contemporary racial attitudes. In P. A. Katz & D. A. Taylor (Eds.), Eliminating racism: Profiles in controversy (pp. 85–116). New York: Plenum.
Boehnke, K. (2001). *Report of the NGO working group on migration and xenophobia for the World Conference on International Migration, Racism, Discrimination and Xenophobia*. A publication jointly produced by ILO, IOM, OHCHR, in consultation with UNHCR.
Boehnke, K., Hagan, J., & Hefler, G. (1998). On the development of xenophobia in Germany: The adolescent years. *Journal of Social Issues, 54*, 585–603.
Bolaffi, G. (Ed.). (2003). *Dictionary of race, ethnicity and culture*. Thousand Oaks, CA: Sage.
Bresnahan, M. J., Ohashi, R., Nebashi, R., Liu, W. Y., & Shearman, S. M. (2002). Attitudinal and affective response toward accented English. *Language and Communication, 22*, 171–185. http://dx.doi.org/10.1016/S0271-5309(01)00025-8.
Brewer, M. B., & Campbell, D. T. (1976). *Ethnocentrism and intergroup attitudes*. New York: Wiley.
Burke, P. (2005). *History and social theory*. Cambridge, UK: Polity.
Cacho, L. M. (2012). *Social death: Racialized rightlessness and the criminalization of the unprotected*. New York, NY: New York University Press.
Cashdan, E. (2001). Ethnocentrism and xenophobia: A cross-cultural study. *Current Anthropology, 42*, 760–765.
Castles, S., & Miller, M. J. (1993). *The age of migration: International population movements in the modern world*. London: Macmillan.

Chavez, L. R. (2001). *Covering immigration: Popular images and the politics of the nation*. Berkeley: University of California Press.

Connely, M. (2006, April 14). In polls, illegal immigrants are called burden. *New York Times*, p. A16.

Creese, G., & Wiebe, B. (2012). 'Survival employment': Gender and deskilling among African immigrants in Canada. *International Migration, 50*(5), 56–76.

Crowther, J. (Ed.). (1995). *Oxford advanced learners dictionary of current English: International new students* (5th ed.). London: Oxford University Press.

Darwin, C. (1859). *On the origin of species: Or, the preservation of favoured races in the struggle for life*. London: Down, Bromley, Kent.

Darwin, C. (1888). *The descent of man and selection in relation to sex*. London: Murray.

Darwin, C. (1898). *The life and letters of Charles Darwin, including an autobiographical chapter* (Rev. ed., F. Darwin, Ed.). London, UK: John Murray.

Dean, J. A., & Wilson, K. (2009). 'Education? It is irrelevant to my job now. It makes me very depressed…': Exploring the health impacts of under/unemployment among highly skilled recent immigrants in Canada. *Ethnicity & Health, 14*(2), 185–204.

de Souza, L. E. C., Pereira, C. R., Camino, L., de Lima, T. J. S., & Torres, A. R. R. (2016). The legitimizing role of accent on discrimination against immigrants. *European Journal of Social Psychology, 46*(5), 609–620.

Dodson, B. (2010). Locating xenophobia: Debate, discourse, and everyday experience in Cape Town, South Africa. *Africa Today, 56*(3), 2–22.

Eckstein, Z., & Weiss, Y. (2004). On the wage growth of immigrants: Israel, 1990–2000. *Journal of the European Economic Association, 2*(4), 665–695.

Edwards, J. (1999). Refining our understanding of language attitudes. *Journal of Language and Social Psychology, 18*, 101–110. http://dx.doi.org/10.1177/0261927X99018001007.

Ervin, N. (1994). Immigration and the environment. In N. Mills (Ed.), *Arguing immigration: Are new immigrants a wealth of diversity… or a crushing burden?* (pp. 90–96). New York: Simon & Schuster.

Espenshade, T. J. (2000). Immigrants, Puerto Ricans, and the earnings of native Black males. In G. D. Jaynes (Ed.), *Immigration and race: New challenges for American democracy* (pp. 125–142). New Haven, CT: Yale University Press.

Esses, V. M., Dovidio, J. F., Jackson, L. M., & Armstrong, T. L. (2001). The immigration dilemma: The role of perceived group competition, ethnic prejudice, and national identity. *Journal of Social Issues, 57*, 389–412.

Esses, V. M., Dovidio, J. F., Semenya, A. H., & Jackson, L. M. (2005). Attitudes toward immigrants and immigration: The role of national and international identity. In D. Abrams, M. A. Hogg, & J. M. Marques, (Eds.), *The social psychology of inclusion and exclusion* (pp. 317–337). New York, NY: Psychology Press.

Fanon, F. (1959/2008). *Black skin/White masks*. New York: Grove Press.

Fernando, S. (1993). Racism and xenophobia. *Innovation: The European Journal of Social Sciences Research, 6*(1), 9–19.

Florack, A., Bless, H., & Piontkowski, U. (2003). When do people accept cultural diversity?: Affect as determinant. *International Journal of Intercultural Relations, 27,* 627–640.

Foner, N., & Fredrickson, G. M. (Eds.). (2004). *Not just Black and White: Historical and contemporary perspectives on immigration, race, and ethnicity in the United States.* New York: Russell Sage Foundation.

Friedman, H. (2009). Xenophilia as a cultural trap: Bridging the gap between transpersonal ... Retrieved from http://psycnet.apa.org/record/2012-07355-010.

Fritzsche, K. (1994). Conditions for xenophobia in eastern Germany (Formerly the GDR). In R. F. Farnen (Ed.), *Nationalism, ethnicity, and identity: Cross national and comparative perspectives* (pp. 277–284). Piscataway, NJ: Transaction Publishers.

Fry, B. N. (2001). *Responding to immigration: Perceptions of promise and threat.* New York: LFB Scholarly Publishers.

Gabaccia, D. R. (2002). *Immigration and American diversity: A concise introduction.* Malden, MA: Blackwell.

Galton, F. (1869). *Hereditary genius: An inquiry into its laws and consequences.* New York: Macmillan.

Galton, F. (1904). Eugenics: Its definition, scope, and aims. *American Journal of Sociology, 10*(1), 1–25.

Gellner, E. (1995). Nationalism and xenophobia. In B. Baumgartl & A. Favell (Eds.), *New xenophobia in Europe* (pp. 6–9). London: Kluwer Law International.

Gluszek, A., & Dovidio, J. F. (2010). Speaking with a nonnative accent: Perceptions of bias, communication difficulties, and belonging in the United States. *Journal of Language and Social Psychology, 29*(2), 224–234.

Guia, A. (2016). The concept of nativism and anti-immigrant sentiments in Europe. *EUI Working Paper, MWP 2016/20.* San Domenico di Fiesoli, Italy: European University Institute. Retrieved on November 4, 2018, from http://cadmus.eui.eu/bitstream/handle/1814/43429/MWP_2016_20.pdf?sequence=1.

Hagendoorn, L., & Sniderman, P. (2001). Experimenting with a national sample: A Dutch survey of prejudice. *Patterns of Prejudice, 35,* 19–31.

Hall, G. S. (1881). *Aspects of German culture.* Boston: J.R. Osgood.

Hansen, K., Rakić, T., & Steffens, M. C. (2017). Foreign-looking native-accented people: More competent when first seen rather than heard. *Social Psychological and Personality Science.* https://doi.org/10.1177/1948550617732389.

Hannaford, I. (1996). *Race: The history of an idea in the West.* Washington, DC: Woodrow Wilson Center Press.

Helms, J. E. (1994). The conceptualization of racial identity and other "racial" concepts. In E. Trickett, R. Watts, & D. Birman (Eds.), *Human diversity: Perspectives on people in context* (pp. 285–311). San Francisco: Jossey-Bass.

Helms, J. E., & Talleyrand, R. M. (1997). Race is not ethnicity. *American Psychologist, 52*, 1246–1247.

Hernandez, R. (1993, March 2). When an accent becomes an issue: Immigrants turn to speech classes to reduce sting of bias. *New York Times*, New York City. Retrieved March 20, 2012, from http://www.nytimes.com/1993/03/02/nyregion/when-accent-becomes-issueimmigrants-turn-speech-classes-reduce-sting-bias.html?pagewanted=all&src=pm.

Higham, J. (1988). *Strangers in the land*. New Brunswick, NJ: Rutgers University Press.

Hosoda, M., & Stone-Romero, E. (2010). The effects of foreign accents on employment-related decisions. *Journal of Managerial Psychology, 25*, 113–132. http://dx.doi.org/10.1108/02683941011019339.

Hovey, J. D., Rojas, R. S., Kain, C., & Magaña, C. (2000). Proposition 187 reexamined: Attitudes toward immigration among California voters. *Current Psychology: Developmental, Learning, Personality, Social, 19*, 159–174.

Jasinskaja-Lahti, I., Liebkind, K., & Perhoniemi, R. (2006). Perceived discrimination and well-being: A victim study of different immigrant groups. *Journal of Community and Applied Social Psychology, 16*, 267–284.

Jaynes, G. D. (Ed.). (2000). *Immigration and race: New challenges for American democracy*. New Haven, CT: Yale University Press.

Jones, K. W. (2001). *Accent on privilege: English identities and Anglophilia in the US*. Philadelphia, PA: Temple University Press.

Kam, C. D., & Kinder, D. R. (2007). Terror and ethnocentrism: Foundations of American support for the war on terrorism. *The Journal of Politics, 69*(2), 320–338.

Kim, C. J. (2000). *Bitter fruit: The politics of Black-Korean conflict in New York City*. New Haven, CT: Yale University Press.

Larsen, L. J. (2004). *The foreign-born population in the United States: 2003* (Current Population Reports, P20-551). Washington, DC: U.S. Census Bureau.

Lee, M. T., Martinez, R., & Rosenfeld, R. (2001). Does immigration increase homicide? Negative evidence from three border cities. *Sociological Quarterly, 42*, 559–580.

Lee, R. G. (2003). *Orientals: Asian American in popular culture*. Philadelphia, PA: Temple University Press.

Lemish, D. (2001). The whore and the other: Israeli images of female immigrants from the former USSR. *Gender & Society, 14*, 333–349.

Lev-Ari, S., & Keysar, B. (2010). Why don't we believe nonnative speakers? The influence of accent on credibility. *Journal of Experimental Social Psychology, 46*, 1093–1096. http://dx.doi.org/10.1016/j.jesp.2010.05.02.

LeVine, R. A., & Campbell, D. T. (1972). *Ethnocentrism: Theories of conflict, ethnic attitudes, and group behavior*. New York: Wiley.

Lin, A. C., & Green, N. W. (2001). *Immigration*. Washington, DC: Division of Congressional Quarterly.
Lorenz, H. S., & Watkins, M. (2001). Silenced knowings, forgotten springs: Paths to healing in the wake of colonialism. *Radical Psychology, 2*(2), 1–19.
Lynn, R. (2001). *Eugenics: A reassessment*. New York: Praeger.
Marger, N. (1997). *Race and ethnic relations: American and global perspective*. New York: International Thompson Publishing.
McClintock, A. (1995). *Imperial leather: Race, gender and sexuality in the colonial contest*. New York: Routledge.
Memmi, A. (2013). *The colonizer and the colonized*. New York: Routledge.
Merriam Webster. (2018). *History of xenophobia*. https://www.merriam-webster.com/words-at-play/a-short-history-of-xenophobia.
Merskin, D. L. (2011). *Media, minorities, and meaning: A critical introduction*. New York: Peter Lang.
Miles, R. (1982). *Racism and migrant labour: A critical text*. London: Routledge.
Misago, J. P., Freemantle, I., & Landau, L. B. (2015). *Protection from xenophobia: An evaluation of UNHCR's regional office for Southern Africa's xenophobia related programmes*. Witwatersrand, South Africa: The African Center for Migration and Society. Retrieved from http://www.unhcr.org/55cb153f9.pdf.
Moradi, B., & Hasan, N. T. (2004). Arab American persons' reported experiences of discrimination and mental health: The mediating role of personal control. *Journal of Counseling Psychology, 51*, 418–428.
Morrison, T. (1994). On the backs of Blacks. In N. Mills (Ed.), *Arguing immigration: Are new immigrants a wealth of diversity... or a crushing burden?* (pp. 97–100). New York: Simon & Schuster.
Navas, M. S. (1998). New measurement instruments for the new racism. *Revista de Psiocologia Social, 13*, 233–239.
Ng, S. H. (2007). Language-based discrimination: Blatant and subtle forms. *Journal of Language and Social Psychology, 26*, 106–122. http://dx.doi.org/10.1177/0261927X07300074.
Ochoa, G. L. (2000). Mexican Americans' attitudes toward and interactions with Mexican immigrants: A qualitative analysis of conflict and cooperation. *Social Science Quarterly, 81*, 84–105.
Pearson, K. (1905). *National life from the standpoint of science*. London: Adam and Black.
Pearson, K. (1911). *The scope and importance to the state of the science of national eugenics*. London: Dulau and Company.
Pedahzur, A., & Yishai, Y. (1999). Hatred by hated people: Xenophobia in Israel. *Studies in Conflict & Terrorism, 22*, 101–117.
Perea, J. F. (1997). Introduction. In J. F. Perea (Ed.), *Immigrants out! The new nativism and the anti-immigrant impulse in the United States* (pp. 1–12). New York: New York University Press.

Pew Hispanic Center. (2016). *Occupations of unauthorized immigrants*. http://www.pewhispanic.org/2016/11/03/occupations-of-unauthorized-immigrant-workers/.

Pinker, S. (2002). *The blank slate: The modern denial of human nature*. New York: Penguin.

Pinker, S. (2018). *Enlightenment now: The case for reason, science, humanism, and progress*. New York: Penguin.

Poole, E., & Richardson, J. E. (Eds.). (2010). *Muslims and the news media*. London, UK: I.B. Tauris.

Pratt, G. (1999). From registered nurse to registered nanny: Discursive geographies of Filipina domestic workers in Vancouver, BC. *Economic Geography, 75*, 215–236.

Rakić, T., Steffens, M. C., & Mummendey, A. (2011). Blinded by the accent! The minor role of looks in ethnic categorization. *Journal of Personality and Social Psychology, 100*, 16–29. http://dx.doi.org/10.1037/a0021522.

Remennick, L. (2005). Immigration, gender, and psychosocial adjustment: A study of 150 immigrant couples in Israel. *Sex Roles, 53*(11–12), 847–863.

Reynolds, V., & Vine, I. (1987). *The socio-biology of ethnocentrism: Evolutionary dimensions of xenophobia, discrimination, racism, and nationalism*. London: Croom Helm.

Rushton, J. P. (1995). *Race, evolution, and behavior.* New Brunswick, NJ: Transaction Publishers.

Schirmer, D. (1998). Introduction. In N. Finzsch & D. Schirmer (Eds.). *Identity and intolerance: Nationalism, racism, and xenophobia in Germany and the United States* (pp. xi–xxxix). Washington, DC: Cambridge University Press.

Segura, D. A. (1989). Chicana and Mexican immigrant women at work: The impact of class, race, and gender on occupational mobility. *Gender & Society, 3*(1), 37–52.

Selden, S. (1999). *Inheriting shame: The story of eugenics and racism in America*. New York: Teachers College Press.

Shamai, S., & Ilatov, Z. (2001). Assimilation and ethnic boundaries: Israeli students' attitudes toward Soviet immigrants. *Adolescence, 36*, 681–695.

Silva, E. B. (2003). *Racism without racists: Color-blind racism and the persistence of racial inequality in the United States*. Lanham, MD: Rowman & Littlefield.

Sloan, T. (2005). Globalization, poverty, and social justice. In G. Nelson & I. Prilleltensky (Eds.), *Community psychology: In pursuit of liberation and well-being* (pp. 309–329). New York: Palgrave.

Smith, J. D. (1985). *Minds made feeble: The myth and legacy of the Kallikaks*. Rockville, MD: Aspen.

Solnit, R. (2004). The Siege of the Sierra Club Anti-immigration ideologues must not be allowed to hijack John Muir's vision. *Mother Jones*. https://www.motherjones.com/environment/2004/03/siege-sierra-club/.

Steiner, E. A. (1909). *The immigrant tide: Its ebb and flow*. New York: F.H. Revell.
Stürmer, S. (2013). *Psychological foundations of xenophilia: The role of major personality*. Retrieved from https://www.ncbi.nlm.nih.gov/pubmed/23834640.
Sue, D. W. (2003). *Overcoming our racism: The journey to liberation*. New York: John Wiley & Sons.
Tactaquin, C. (1998). The greening of the anti-immigrant agenda. *Network News*, Spring Issue.
Taggart, P. (2000). *Populism*. Buckingham: Open University Press.
Taras, R. (2012). *Xenophobia and Islamophobia in Europe*. Edinburgh, UK: Edinburgh University Press.
The Institute for Women's Policy Research. (2018). *Imigrant women*. Retrieved June 19, 2018 from https://statusofwomendata.org/immigrant-women/.
Thornton, M. C., & Mizuno, Y. (1999). Economic well-being and Black adult feelings toward immigrants and Whites, 1984. *Journal of Black Studies, 30*, 15–44.
Tucker, W. H. (1996). *The science and politics of racial research*. Urbana-Champaign, IL: University of Illinois Press.
UNHCR. (2001). *International migration, racism, discrimination and xenophobia*. A Publication Jointly Produced by the International Labor Organization, International Organization for Migration, and the Office of the United Nations High Commisioner for Human Rights. Geneva, Switzerland: The UN Nigh Commissioner for Refugees. Retrieved November 2, 2018, from https://www2.ohchr.org/english/issues/migration/taskforce/docs/wcar.pdf.
Waldinger, R. (1997). Black/immigrant competition re-assessed: New evidence from Los Angeles. *Sociological Perspectives, 40*, 365–386.
Waldinger, R., Ward, R., & Aldrich, H. (1985). Ethnic business and occupational mobility in advanced societies. *Sociology, 19*(4), 586–597.
Watts, M. W. (1996). Political xenophobia in the transition from socialism: Threat, racism and ideology among East German youth. *Political Psychology, 17*, 97–126.
Wimmer, A. (1997). Explaining xenophobia and racism: A critical review of current research approaches. *Ethnic and Racial Studies, 20*, 17–41.
Wistrich, R. S. (2011). *Demonizing the other: Antisemitism, racism, and xenophobia*. London, UK: Routledge.
Wolfram, W., & Schilling-Estes, N. (2006). *American English: Dialects and Variation* (2nd ed.). Malden and Oxford: Blackwell.
Yakushko, O. (2009b). Xenophobia: Understanding the roots and consequences of negative attitudes towards immigrants. *The Counseling Psychologist, 37*, 36–66.
Yakushko, O. (2010a). Stress and coping strategies in the lives of recent immigrants: A grounded theory model. *International Journal for the Advancement of Counselling, 32*(4), 256–273.

Yakushko, O. (2010b). Working through interpreters with limited-English proficiency clients: A phenomenological investigation. *Professional Psychology: Research, Theory, and Practice, 41*(5), 449–455.

Yakushko, O., & Blodgett, E. (2018). Immigration. *Handbook of Multicultural Psychology.*

Yakushko, O., & Morgan-Consoli, M. L. (2012). Immigration: Research, clinical practice and training. In N. Fouad & J. Carter (Eds.). *The handbook of counseling psychology.* Thousand Oaks: Sage.

Young, R. J. (2005). *Colonial desire: Hybridity in theory, culture and race.* New York: Routledge.

Zinn, H. (2010). *The twentieth century: A people's history.* New York: Harper & Row.

Zizek, S. (1997). *The plague of fantasies.* London: Verso.

CHAPTER 3

The Immigrant Tides: Xenophobia in Western History Xenophobia as Neither Universal Nor Historically Invariable

Abstract Recent Western history is marked by waves of migration based on political and social changes, including histories of wars, colonization, and capitalist trade route developments. This chapter discusses this history as well as anti-immigrant reactions, legitimized through Inquisition, anti-Semitic movements, eugenics, colonialism, and capitalist globalization and political developments.

Keywords History · The witch hunts · Colonialism · Eugenics · Globalization

Xenophobia, like colonial racism or patriarchy, is neither universal nor biologically invariable as evident in human history or contemporary human societies. Despite proclamations that hatred and dislike of strangers or foreigners is universal, biological, and historically invariable, evidence from archeological and anthropological accounts points to the predominance of societies that were open to outsiders. Archeological evidence suggests that peoples of the Middle East, indigenous tribes of North America, or the Mediterranean point to significant influence of cultural exchanges, intermarriages, and cross-group collaborations (Carballo, Roscoe, & Feinman, 2014; Haynes, 2000; Lyons & Clark, 2008; McClintock, 1995; Pritzker, 2000; Stein, 2002). Interregional and intercultural exchanges, especially for purposes of trade, have been shown to be one of the most common parts of the human cultural

O. Yakushko, *Modern-Day Xenophobia*,
https://doi.org/10.1007/978-3-030-00644-0_3

history: immigrant or foreign diasporas could be marginalized by their host communities although diasporas' autonomous and even dominant roles have been documented to be just as frequent (Curtin, 1984; Kivisto & Faist, 2009; Lyons & Clark, 2008; Stein, 2002).

Historical Causes of Human Migrations

Movement of people across borders had multiple internal and external causes. Certainly, through history individuals moved because of wanderlust and desire for new experiences. However, in recent history majority of individuals relocated their homes and families to new lands in search of better economic opportunities, greater religious freedom, or escape from socially traumatizing events such as wars (Kivisto & Faist, 2009). Western history because of its preoccupations with control and dominance over resources, including human beings, is marked by periods of xenophobia toward the newcomers (Dodson, 2010; Gabaccia, 2002; Gellner, 1995; Jung, 2004; Licata & Klein, 2002; Oakley, 1996; Perea, 1997; Pettigrew, 1998; Vale, 2002). These periods often follow historical phases with significant conflict or colonization between a host country and other nations or during consolidation of supposedly fragile national identity (Art, 2017; Licata & Klein, 2002; Perea, 1997). For example, anti-immigrant prejudice toward Japanese and Germans during mid-twentieth century U.S. was precipitated by World War II national divides (Aruga, 1994; Daniels, 1977). Many Western European nations engaged in long periods of brutal occupation and imperial colonization of North African nations, which are now the most common countries of origin for immigrants and refugees to Europe (Fanon, 1959/2008; Licata & Klein, 2002; Memmi, 2013).

Ignoring these historical facts further facilitates the denial of underlying social factors that create social instabilities, establish social categories (i.e., fit and unfit races, developed and undeveloped nations) that generate both the demand for migrant labor as well as conditions that make life unlivable without relocation. Said (1993), a post-colonial scholar, emphasized that cultural social theories must be grounded in the concept of what he termed the cultural archive, which emphasize the central role of Western imperialism on contemporary history. According to Williamson (1997), imperialism and colonization of non-Western nations underlie many causes of world migration:

> what is now known as the Third World [sic] were segmented by discrimination, language, and custom. They were segmented by long distance and high costs. They were segmented by the poverty of the Third World labor surplus areas, areas so poor that potential emigrants would have found it impossible to finance the move to the booming OECD labor markets anyway. (pp. 117–118)

Bosma (2007) further expanded discussion of the history of imperialism and colonial occupations, stating that European and Western cultures as well as their scholars sought to create sanitized versions of "pull" theories of immigration, which implied the presence of "free" flow of labor by individuals who "freely" chose such relocations. According to Bosma's theories in relation to "the causes of segmentation of labor markets and their concomitant compartmentalization of migration flows" show evidence of the racist historical narratives that claim

> These [immigrant labor movements] did not emerge naturally, but involved numerous government decisions to control migration. My contention would be that these mechanisms of control were, consciously or unconsciously, increasingly navigated by a social Darwinist mindset. What I mean is the implicit or explicit assumption that there is a "hierarchy of human races" in terms of their propensity to operate in modern civilization. In this hierarchy black labour was enslaved, Asian labour indentured, whereas the apex was firmly held by the free white well-educated northern European. Since government decisions were informed by this racial taxonomy, it became ingrained in migration history. (p. 117)

In addition, Casey and Watkins (2014) documented that tremendous anti-Mexican xenophobia developed in California following the violent annexation of lands and property from Mexicans following Mexican–American war. In addition, increase in migration often occurs when host country appears to have increased labor needs, whether it is for highly specialized occupations such as technical or scientific jobs or, more commonly, for low level-low-cost labor (Bauder, 2003; Bosma, 2007; Chavez, 2001; Perea, 1997; Sloan, 2005). In fact, multiple studies have shown that immigration results in an increase in the GDP of the host countries without negatively affecting earning potential or access to jobs of the native-born individuals (Addison & Worswick, 2002; Ortega & Peri, 2009). Moreover, Johnson (1980) showed that immigration increases, rather than decreases, the earning potential of both the host country's high skills workers and owners of the capital without reducing the income of its native-born earners. Immigrants contribute to creation of new trade routes or connections as well as to flow of capital between the home and host cultures, often resulting in financial benefits primarily for the host community (Head & Ries, 1998). Presence of newcomers has been repeatedly shown to decrease crime (Lee & Martinez, 2009; Ousey & Kurbin, 2009). These beneficial aspects of migration for the host nation often implicitly encourage such migration (e.g., the brain drain, low-cost labor) although simultaneously they also produce explicit xenophobic narratives about the very same benefits is that immigrants and migration are a threat (e.g., jobs taken from native-born individuals). Thus, the history of xenophobia is the history of marginalized foreign diasporas or foreigners that have distinct sociohistorical antecedents.

Historic Xenophobic Treatment of Jews and Other Foreigners in Europe

One of the most documented histories of such marginalization, exclusion and violence is toward Jewish individuals, often treated and perceived as perpetual foreigners and strangers, especially in Christianized Europe (Wistrich, 2011). During medieval and Enlightenment eras, European Jews were often demonized and represented as a danger to dominant community, often blamed for economic recessions, plagues, rise in sexual immorality, and other cultural declines (Yakushko, 2018b; Yuval, 2011). For example, one of the most infamous books, considered the bloodiest book ever written, *The Malleus Malleficarum (The Witches Hammer)*, often casts the blame for demonic possessions and influences on Jews:

> For we read in the *Lives of the Fathers*, that a certain girl would not consent to a young man who was begging her to commit a shameful act with him. And the young man, being angry because of this, caused a certain Jew to work a charm against her, by which she was changed into a filly. (*The Malleus Malleficarum*, Part I, Question X)

Moreover, Jews are charged with religious and cultural infidelity and sins against the faith, blaming them as a source of demonic influences on faithful Christians across Europe:

> the Jews sin more greatly than the Pagans; for they received the prophecy of the Christian Faith in the Old Law, which they corrupt through badly interpreting it, which is not the case with the Pagans. Therefore their infidelity is a greater sin than that of the Gentiles, who never received the Faith of the Gospel. (*The Malleus Malleficarum*, Part I, Question XIV)

Jews were not the only foreign targets of these persecutions. The Inquisition frequently focused on demonic presence and influences of any foreigner or being exposed to one, because their potential pagan or non-Christian inclinations were viewed as dangerous to morals and health of Christian European society.

> Asked where he was brought up, and where he chiefly lived, he answered, in such or such a place. And if it appears that he has changed abode because, perhaps, his mother or any of his kindred was not suspected, and had lived in foreign districts, especially in such places as are most frequented by witches, he shall be questioned accordingly. (*The Malleus Malleficarum*, Part III, Second Head, Question VI)

Thus, historically European xenophobia as related to prejudice toward Jews and other foreigners, often focusing on their religious, cultural, and moral unsuitability and supposedly their demonic threat to dominant European communities. Notably, Jews as well as other foreigners (e.g., Moors) were a diasporic immigrant community (i.e., native-born in nations or states, in which they resided) (Wistrich, 2011).

Historical Role of Xenophobia in Enslavement of People

Another visible way in which xenophobia functioned in history is evident in periods of forced migration of people groups, which were enslaved or indentured as free or low-paid wage labor (Bosma, 2007; Zinn, 2010). Enslaving people who were indeed foreign rather than native-born and then maintaining their alien and dehumanized status, including by denying them citizenship or any rights of the native-born, functioned to create highly lucrative systems of labor as well as a social space for projecting cultural negative attributes into them such as violence (Baldwin, 1993;

Fanon, 1959/2008; Williamson, 1997; Zinn, 2010). It is notable that demand for extremely cheap labor from individuals who could be considered sub- or non-human and as a cultural threat dramatically increased in Europe and the United States after these Western nations outlawed formal slavery and decreased colonial occupations, thus encouraging migration (Cacho, 2000; Fanon, 1959/2008; Kivisto & Faist, 2009; Memmi, 2013). A contemporary form of forced migration is found in human trafficking for sexual and labor exploitation, further complicating patterns and boundaries of what constitutes migration as during historical periods of slavery and colonial occupations (Bales & Soodalter, 2010; Gozdziak & Collett, 2005; Yakushko, 2009a).

Xenophobic Determinants of Unfitness: Social Darwinism and Eugenics in Modern History

Another recent demonization of immigrants as a threat is visible in the history of Europe, the United States and other politically dominant nations that embraced social Darwinism and eugenics as a framework for the treatment of immigrants as threatening intruders. As noted earlier, Darwin (1859, 1888, 1898) frequently discussed differences between supposedly human "races" that were represented by national groups, elevating Nordic and Aryan groups to the status of the evolutionary fit, whose superiority was not only evident in their intelligence, happiness, and cultural artifacts whereas uncivilized races were now statistically shown to be marked by lower intelligence, sexual immorality, unhealth, and emotional volatility (Bashford & Levine, 2010; Black, 2003; Lombardo, 2011; McClintock, 1995; Merskin, 2011; Yakushko, in review). Eugenics or the "science of racial betterment" operated primarily through identifying and promoting the survival of the supposedly fittest groups and individuals while insuring that the unfit were eliminated, either directly or through policies of segregation and sterilization after being assessed for their evolutionary fitness (Davenport, 1910; Galton, 1865, 1869, 1883, 1904; Goddard, 1911, 1912, 1914, 1917; Hall, 1903, 1909, 1917a, b; Lynn, 2001; McDougall, 1921; Pearson, 1905, 1911; Terman, 1916). All foreigners who were perceived as arriving from supposedly "uncivilized" countries (i.e., China, India) or, in Emma Lazarus s' terms "the wretched refuse of your [cilized superior countries] teeming shore" (i.e., Jews from Germany), represented an evolutionary threat (Bashford & Levine, 2010; Lombardo, 2011; Tucker, 1996). Every single eugenic book and journal produced in the United States and the U.K. had dedicated sections on the menace of immigration and eugenic solution to this problem (e.g., Brigham, 1923; *Eugenical Review*, 1916–1922; McDougall, 1921; Popenoe & Johnson, 1918/1935). Eugenic organizations included separate committees on eugenic "solutions" to immigration, and governments included Committees on immigration "problems" (*Eugenical News*, 1916–1922). For example, Howard Crosby Warren, an American psychologist and the president of the American Psychological Association in 1913 also was a leader in the American Eugenic Research Association as well as the Expert Eugenic Agent on the U.S. House Committee on Immigration and Naturalization. Raymond Dodge, another top American psychologist and the president of the American Psychological Association in 1916, was a dedicated eugenicist who founded the National Research Council's Committee on Problems of Human Migration (Yakushko, in review). Notably, in these eugenicists efforts Jews, viewed as perpetual foreigners, were rebranded as the evolutionary unfit rather than demonically possessed, and scientific eugenic programs instituted in the Nazi Germany produced what we now know as the Holocaust were fueled by British and American eugenic sciences (Kuhl, 2002; Weikart, 2004). Jews feeling the Holocaust were denied entry to the United States because of their supposed feeble-mindedness and lack of evolutionary fitness (Smith, 1985; Tucker, 1996).

Moreover, in many American and British professions such as psychology "Jewish" influences were considered reflective of racial unfitness (e.g., amorality, avariciousness). Thus, psychoanalysis was often dismissed and maligned for this reason, with academic positions being denied to psychoanalytic scholars who were suspect of being under such "foreign" Influence (Frosh, 2004; Yakushko, in review). For example, Stanley G. Hall (1917a, b), a founding member of American academic psychology and the first president of the American Psychological Association and leader of U.S. eugenic organizations, pronounced that psychoanalysis was dangerous because its non-eugenic focus encouraged individuals to plunge down the supposed evolutionary ladder. Thus, eugenics with its distinct xenophobic and anti-Semitic focus had significant influence on professional, occupational, and even theoretical scope of.

Thus, for individuals from dominant Western countries, presenting themselves being populated by predominately evolutionary fit individuals who were working toward becoming utopian Master races (Davenport, 1910; McDougall, 1921), immigrants were perceived to be a significant threat because of the immigrants' evolutionary unfitness, now proved through scientific studies rather than religious edicts (Brigham, 1923; Pearson, 1905, 1911; Popenoe & Johnson, 1918/1935). In both the United States and Britain, measurement of intelligence and personality became paramount as a mark appropriate germo-plasm or genetic material that would contribute to eugenic (development) rather than dysgenic (destruction) of these cultures through evidence of intelligence, optimism, self-control, and other evolutionary superior characteristics (Bashford & Levine, 2010; Lombardo, 2011).

The United States and the Northern European politicians and the media of the early twentieth century expressed specific concern in relation to migration of Jews, Slavs, and the South Europeans across their border. Davenport (1910), Harvard University biologist and a leader of American eugenicists, pronounced in his popular book *Heredity in Relation to Eugenics* that immigration is a threat to the United states

> on account of the recent influx of immigrants from Southeastern Europe, rapidly become darker in pigmentation, smaller in stature, more mercurial, more attached to music and art, more given to crimes of larceny, kidnapping, assault murder, rape, and sex-immorality and less given to burglary, drunkness, and vagrancy than were the original English settlers. (p. 219)

American psychologists who occupied top academic posts and led the American Psychological Association and other professional academic societies became leaders of eugenic testing practices with immigrants. According to Yerkes (1923), a Harvard psychologist, two-time president of the American Psychological Association, editor of top psychology journals and leader of multiple eugenic organizations, "eugenics, the art of breeding better men, imperatively demands reliable measurement of human traits of body and mind" (p. 225). Among the most influential of such eugenic studies were the Army Mental Tests, conducted on almost two million U.S. Army personnel in the early twentieth century (Tucker, 1996). Promoted as unbiased and unquestioningly scientific, these studies produced stunning racist results such as claiming that almost all African American recruits possessed lowest levels of intelligence (Brigham, 1923; Yerkes, 1923).

However, just as pronounced were the xenophobic results of these studies. Brigham (1923), a Princeton psychologist, known as the developer of the Scholastic Apprehension Test (SAT), proclaimed in the highly popularized summary of these tests entitled *A Study in American Intelligence* that "our figures... tend to disprove the popular belief that the Jew is highly intelligent" (p. 190). These findings further expounded popular eugenic writings by top academics such as Davenport (1910) that their studies showed that:

> The Hebrews showed the greatest proportion of crimes against chastity ... there is no question that, taken as a whole, the hordes of Jews that are coming to us... with their intense individualism and ideals of gain at the cost of any interest, represent the opposite extreme from the early English and more recent Scandinavian immigration with their ideals of community life in the open country, advancement by the sweat of the brow, and the uprearing of families in the fear of God and the love of country. (p. 216)

Brigham (1923) further summarized that "Army tests of foreign-born individuals have pointed at every step to the conclusion that the average intelligence of our immigrants is declining" (p. 197), claiming that "no doubt... [immigrants are] intellectually closer to the negro than to the native-born white sample" (p. 199). Therefore, eugenicists such as Yerkes (1923) admonished the American public, "to consider their [study results] reliability and their meaning" in order to address "the menace of race deterioration or the evident relations of immigration to national progress and welfare" (p. viii). Using these and other eugenic scientific results, politicians were called to "only to admit those who are superior to the median American in mental endowment as far as this is shown by approved mental tests" (Evans, 1931, p. 16). *A Study in American Intelligence* (1923) urged for "legal steps... be taken...[to] insure a continually progressive upward evolution" (p. 210) including through closing borders, testing all immigrants with intelligence and personality measures, and building barriers on the Southern border. Among numerous scholarly and theoretical articles related to dangers of immigration for the United states, the primary eugenic publication produced by the Eugenic Record Office *Eugenical News* (1928) decried "the alarming influx of Mexican Peons [who] inject another serious color problem into American life" (v13, p. 24).

Treatment of many foreign groups in the United States provides similar evidence of supposed threat to the majority of White wealthy Americans: the Yellow Peril and the Chinese Exclusionary acts to focus on the supposed menace by Asian immigrants; supposed flood of Mexican "peons" over the southern borders; and the economic and cultural threat (especially through "over-population") by the Irish, Russian, Italian, Polish, or Hungarian immigrants (Bashford & Levine, 2010; *The Eugenic News*, 1916–1922; Lombardo, 2011; Merskin, 2011). Goddard (1911, 1912, 1917), an infamous eugenicists who produced scientific foundations for sterilization and abusive treatment of all those perceived as feeble-minded (i.e., tested by psychologists to have borderline intelligence as also evidenced by their poverty, non-normative sexuality, ethnicity, race, and disabilities), was also involved in development of intelligence and personality testing of immigrants at the Ellis and other ports of entry to the United States According to Smith (1985), Goddard trained his testing para-professionals to wander between newly arriving immigrants at the port entries and identify them by supposedly problematic emotional behaviors, which apparently belied their low intelligence and morality. The common manner of testing immigrants, according to Goddard's descriptions, was to pull them out of waiting lines to be tested, consistently finding that they were feeble-minded or morons (Smith, 1985). These results were praised to the public, the government, and academic authorities as highly scientific and accurate (Tucker, 1996). Goddard (1917) boasted that at the "beginning… [of] experiment, the number of aliens deported because of feeble-mindedness… increased approximately 350 percent in 1913 and 570 percent in 1914 over what it had been in each of the five proceeding years" (p. 271). Goddard (1911, 1912, 1917) was known for promoting eventual elimination of all the feeble-minded, their use for hard labor in segregated camps, their sterilization, and removal of voting rights in order to establish eugenic aristo-democracy by supposedly evolutionary fit. His testing of immigrants produced studies that proved that over 80% of Jews, Slavs, Italians, Hungarians, and other non-Nordic immigrants, were supposedly feeble-minded and should be barred entry to the United states (Goddard, 1917).

Many American politicians and cultural leaders openly embraced eugenics in relation to immigrant groups. Theodore Roosevelt, who was committed to eugenics, routinely supported closing of the borders and denial of services to recent immigrants, especially insisting on their complete assimilation. T. Roosevelt, for example, provided endorsement for eugenic books about promoting creation of the Master Race such as Grant Madison's (1921) *The Passing of the Great Race*, stating that "Americans should be sincerely grateful to [Grant] for writing it" (cover). **Roosevelt further quipped**, "There is no room in this country for hyphenated Americanism. ...The one absolutely certain way of bringing this nation to ruin, of preventing all possibility of its continuing to be a nation at all, would be to permit it to become a tangle of squabbling nationalities" (Address to Knights of Columbus, October 12, 1915). Another one of his requirements was that "every immigrant who comes here should be required within five years to learn English or leave the country" (Roosevelt, 1894, online).

Calvin Coolidge, another president who operated during the height of eugenic political and cultural dominance in the United States, marked by immigration restrictions for all non-Nordic immigrants, proclaimed importance of testing immigrants for their supposed fitness to be part of civic American life:

> American institutions rest solely on good citizenship. They were created by people who had a background of self-government. New arrivals should be limited to our capacity to absorb them into the ranks of good citizenship. America must be kept American. For this purpose, it is necessary to continue a policy of restricted immigration. It would lie well to make such immigration of a selective nature with some inspection at the source, and based either on a prior census or upon the record of naturalization. Either method would insure the admission of those with the largest capacity and best intention of becoming citizens. I am convinced that our present economic and social conditions warrant a limitation of those to be admitted. We should find additional safety in a law requiring the immediate registration of all aliens. Those who do not want to be partakers of the American spirit ought not to settle in America. (First Message to Congress, December 1923)

In addition, other cultural leaders routinely emphasized eugenics as a solution to their country's social problems. While instituting racial school segregation, eugenic leaders also promoted universal education not because it was a human right but because it would permit all children to be tested and segregated as well as vocationally tracked based on their evolutionary fitness levels (Black, 2003; Selden, 1999). Privileged young women were encouraged to gain some college education (though never advanced or in so-called masculine occupations) because their presence in colleges would encourage their pairing with evolutionary fit men, make them ready to be mother's of next generation of evolutionary fit, and preventing men from turning to each other for sexual relationships (Popenoe & Johnson, 1918/1935). Evolutionary fit was encouraged to follow diets of the superior races (i.e., North European diet) such as the eugenic Flow Diet promoted by the cereal mogul and eugenicist Kellogg (Cogdell, 2010; Currell & Cogdell, 2006). Early feminist American leaders such as Margaret Sanger (1919, 1921) justified their fight for women's reproductive rights through openly eugenic xenophobic rhetoric, posing that on one hand there was a "population decline" (i.e., fewer children born of eugenically fit) while at the same time decrying "overpopulation" (i.e., too many children born by eugenically unfit, primarily by Jews and southern Europeans). Sanger like other leaders claiming to be feminist, argued for sterilization especially of all the non-Nordic immigrants because once sterilized, these individuals would pose less threat to morals and health of its native-born privileged population (Black, 2003; Sanger, 1919, 1921).

Immigrants were often pitted against native-born minorities who struggled for access to economic resources and social services, especially African Americans whose experiences following the Emancipation proclamation continued to be marked by extreme forms of oppression and social violence (Black, 2003; Du Bois, 1903). For instance, Frederick Douglass, an abolitionist and social leader noted that

> The old employments by which we have heretofore gained our livelihood, are gradually, and it may seem inevitably, passing into other hands. Every hour sees the black man elbowed out of employment by some newly arrived immigrant whose hunger and whose color are thought to give him a better title to the place. (Speech Delivered before the A. A. S. Society, in New York, May, 1853)

Thus, immigration of non-Aryan groups to Britain, Germany, and the USA was proclaimed as a primary reason for governments to establish national eugenic policies. According to Saleeby (1911)

> migration accounts for the disproportionate increase of [evolutionary unfit] population in the United States. But it may be added that the imminent arrest or control of this immigration will assuredly have the most serious and pressing consequences for Europe. Plainly it must hasten the coming of national eugenics. (pp. 76–77)

Karl Pearson (1905, 1911, 1930), a eugenicist, a Darwinist, and a founder of the field of statistics whose empirical work focused almost exclusively on social Darwinist and eugenic determinations of human fitness. In his 1930 book that documented Galton's eugenic legacy noted that eugenicists, like Galton, recognized that at times "great men" migrated because they felt persecuted in their own lands or that some immigrants groups could contribute to so-called racially advanced cultures. Pearson noted that although Galton was continually concerned about the detrimental impact of immigration, he also stated that if immigrants improved "civic worth, whether it be one of brains or energy, artistic power or skill," such immigrants should be welcomed while denying entry to the "undesirables" (p. 229).

Furthermore, native-born individuals were routinely warned against sexual relations with foreigners because of potential passing on the parasitic hereditary characteristic to next generations, who would be considered native-born. According to Pearson's (1930) summary of Galton's eugenic work in *The Life, Letters, and Labours of Francis Galton*:

> What Galton says about British physique and about the physical beauty of our trunk and limbs is probably very true. We have recently seen the foreigner our equal or even our superior at most of our national sports; he only needed the proper training to defeat us. Nor is the somewhat low standard of physical beauty confined to trunk and limbs—anyone who makes an extensive study of the English skull must be forced to the conclusion that aesthetically at least it is not of a high type. The stock-breeder "looking over the hedge" must conclude that these are not directions in which much can easily be achieved. Yet he would affirm emphatically and "with justice that the whole of a race which was able to furnish the large supply which is produced in Great Britain of men who are sound in body, capable in mind, energetic and of high character, has the capacity (speaking as a rearer of stock) of being raised to at least the same high level." (p. 253)

Certainly, miscegenation laws against foreigners, including Jews in Nazi Germany or the Chinese in the United States were based on the same eugenic xenophobic rhetoric (Black, 2003; Kuhl, 2002; McClintock, 1995; Weikart, 2004).

Recent History of Xenophobia: Fantasizing Immigrant Threats and Fetishizing Immigrants

Contemporary American and European evidence of xenophobia is well documented (Gibson, 2002; Merskin, 2011; Perea, 1997; Taras, 2012; Yakushko, 2009a, b). In addition to rhetoric continually delivered by the current U.S. president and many far-right politicians around the globe, the media, and other culturally influential agencies promote views of immigrants as dangerous "aliens," "animals," and "criminals" (Ana, 1999; Chavez, 2001; Merskin, 2011). Continued emphasis is placed on supposed danger immigrants pose to physical health of native-born majority, including by representing them as infected with AIDS or leprosy. In 2005 Lou Dobbs, then part of CNN, stated that "The invasion of illegal aliens is threatening the health of many Americans," evoking leprosy as one such threat (Leonhardt, 2007). Immigrants to Western countries, especially undocumented immigrants, are experiencing significantly higher levels of violent hate crimes, violations of their rights, employment mistreatment, and denial of access to services (Merskin, 2011; Yakushko, 2009a, b).

Immigrants, whether legal or illegal, are continually represented as a threat through repeated propagation of myths and stereotypes. For example, in the United states immigrants are portrayed as "illegal," as costing jobs of native-born individuals, as being criminal, as refusing to learn English, as being a significant social burden, as being terrorists, as well as being uneducated and sick (Teaching Tolerance, 2011). The facts that are avoided in discourse on immigrants include the fact that less than 12% of all immigrants in the United states entered the country without documents (Lopez & Radford, 2017); over 56% of recent immigrants speak English "well" or "very well" (Gambino, Acosta, & Grieco, 2014); immigrants have much lower rate of criminal behavior and incarceration than native-born individuals, and in fact greater number of immigrants in a community appears to reduce crime and violence (Shiochet, 2015); and rather than being an economic burden, undocumented immigrants alone contributed $13 billion through taxes alone (Goss et al., 2013). According to Nowrasteh (2016), it is more than 250 times more likely to be murdered by native-born individual than a foreign-born terrorist, even though the rhetoric of many politicians focus on immigration as a terrorist threat.

Among the most common damages often assigned to immigrants is their impact on jobs and the economy. According to the report published by the American Immigration Council (2013), there is (1) no relationship (no correlation) between levels of immigration and unemployment, (2) evidence that native-born and foreign-born individuals do not compete for the same jobs, (3) no relationship (no correlation) between immigration and unemployment among native-born ethnic or racial minorities, and (4) evidence that immigration contributes to creation of new jobs. These facts, as noted earlier, like the representation of foreigners as being possessed by demonic powers or as carrying parasitic germo-plasms that damaged evolution of others, point to the creation and perpetuation of xenophobia based on prejudicial and non-factual fabrications.

Immigrants' cause in social decline and great social costs gained new dimensions. During the eugenics era the supposed overpopulation by unfit immigrants caused problematic declines in morality and overall intelligence of the fit privileged Western peoples as well as contributing to declines in physical and mental health (Brigham, 1923; Davenport, 1910; Popenoe & Johnson, 1918/1935). In contrast, the new threat of the overpopulation by immigrants is supposedly the main cause of negative environmental changes. For example, groups that emphasize restriction of immigration often use the overpopulation of immigrants arguments, such as the Zero Population Growth and the Californians for Population Stabilization (Connelly, 2006). The Californians for Population Stabilization routinely proclaim that California's environmental problems such as recent drought are the result of state's high population of immigrants who "take too many showers" (Californians for Population Stabilization, 2018; Linthicum, 2015). At one time, even such reputable organizations as Sierra Club used xenophobic anti-immigrant rhetoric in their statements about environmental issues (Ervin, 1994; Solnit, 2004; Tactaquin, 1998).

Like with sexism and patriarchy, another potential evidence of xenophobia can be found in fetishizing and commodifying immigrants. Sexist and patriarchal representation of women focuses on either their position as happy housewives and mothers or as sexually dangerous mad ingrates, either as Madonnas or as Whores (Unger & Crawford, 1992). Both representations highlight a dehumanized fetishized version of women and girls. Similarly, contemporary xenophobic rhetoric splits immigrants into "model minorities" who are smart and compliant versus "gangs;" or as perfect "international brides" versus scheming prostitutes; or as industrious reliable laborers versus criminal cheats; violent animals deserving of the enslavement or "Master's children" (Merskin, 2011).

Like with race and gender categories, explicit use of emotional states as categories of social control also reflect xenophobic viewpoints that shape attitudes toward immigrants (Ahmed, 2013; Merskin, 2011; Yakushko, 2018a). Eugenicists of the early twentieth century routinely focused on supposedly problematic morality and emotional tendencies of feeble-minded immigrants. Wiggam (1923) in the highly popular book on eugenics entitled the *New Decalogue of Science* decried such common personality traits among the evolutionary unfit as their "high temper, uncontrollable fits of anger, feebleness of will, inability to hold a social ideal permanently in mind, lack of ambition to provide as good homes as their neighbors… and mental 'drive'" (p. 58). Goddard (1917), who established eugenic intelligence and personality testing of immigrants at U.S. port entries published concerns about failures to assess and refuse entry/deport entry to those who may have passed intelligence testing but still lacked requisite docility and submissiveness. In his work detailing his immigration work Goddard (1917) discussed a working-class immigrant Irish woman, whom he described as having been found "intelligent" but still problematic because "there was about this girl a certain obstinacy, a determination to do her own way… [a] peculiar mental state [that] seemed incurable" (p. 265).

More recently, scholars have noted that the coverage of the Holocaust and Jewish experience in the U.S. post-World War II quickly focused away on the horrors of surviving torture to celebrating those Jews who were supposedly resilient (unlike their counterparts who struggled or committed suicide) and even grew from their experiences (i.e., torture made them stronger) (Danieli, 1984). Danieli (1985) proposed the term "conspiracy of silence" in regard to cultural incapacity to attend to the Holocaust experiences:

> Survivors' war accounts were too horrifying for most people to listen to or believe. Additionally, bystanders' guilt led many to regard the survivors as pointing accusing fingers at them. Survivors were also faced with the pervasively held myth that they had actively or passively participated in their own destiny by "going like sheep to the slaughter," and with the suspicion that they had performed immoral acts in order to survive. Reactions such as these ensured the survivors' silence about their Holocaust experiences. (p. 296)

In contemporary times other than occasional account of severe trauma experienced by an immigrant, which they heroically overcame, most recent migrants appear to be expected to just be happy about being permitted to live in Western countries, and if they dare to complain about their past or present circumstance, are told to either put the past behind them or "go back home to where they came from" (Yakushko, 2009a, b). The current rhetoric emphasizes the post-traumatic growth, which demands that whatever past and present traumas and challenges immigrants have experienced either must result in their improved meaning and functioning or face being blamed for yet another incapacity to function like the optimistic native-born people (Yakushko, 2018a). These aspects of xenophobic emphasis on controlling emotions are especially visible in contemporary positive psychology, which relies on denying the role of history and social context (i.e., learned helplessness is derived from lack of internal attributions) (Yakushko, 2018a). Thus, although Mexican Americans are among the most openly vilified and marginalized ethnic immigrant groups in the United States, they are proclaimed to be the happiest and used as an emotional model minority (Yakushko, 2018a). In these objectified narratives, immigrants are often denied their full humanity, whether emotional (i.e., reality of traumatic reactions in face of violence or access of a full range of emotions in reactions to complex human experiences) or social (i.e., immigrants are either silent hard workers/housewives or violent gang members). In addition, continued representation of immigrants as "tired" and "poor" as well as "the wretched refuse of your [other countries] teeming shore" (Lazarus, 1883), while evoking supposedly humanitarian responses, may further serve to dehumanize immigrants and evoke resentment among the native-born. Similarly, Black people are routinely represented as gullible and bighearted on one hand while violent and impulsive on another, or women as coy and helpless while also nagging and angry, or indigenous people as naïve and passive as well as merciless and vicious uses stereotyped ideologies to further degrade, control, and diminish minority groups (Ahmed, 2013; Merskin, 2011). Throughout American history minorities, including immigrants, have been fetishized as Mammies, Chiefs, Uncle Toms, Banditos/Gang Members, Gurus, Cantina Girls, Science Nerds, and Geishas, conscripting and constraining human beings into narrow stereotyped categories (Merskin, 2011).

Xenophobic emphases on immigrants' muteness about their past and present traumatic experiences together with requirement of strict emotional control and cheerfulness lead to silencing immigrants, including when they are routinely accused of being a danger and a threat to the native-born if they are upset, angry, or sad. Immigrants are still rejected from entering because of perceptions of their individual or collective supposed emotional instability or at the very least perceived as costing Western countries untold money in services. The media routinely promotes stories of individual immigrants who triumphed over their terrible fate. And dominant psychology movements emphasize concepts such as resilience, post-traumatic growth (rather than trauma), primacy of internalized attributions, and once again, heredity and genetics (Yakushko, 2018a). Normative reactions to immigration, and considerable traumatic events that precipitate them, are silenced and shamed for being too socially costly. According to Duggan (2012), these emphases reflect neoliberal or fundamentalist capitalist Western assumptions, which have "promoted 'private' competitions, self-esteem and independence as the roots of personal responsibility, and excoriated 'public' entitlement, dependency, and irresponsibility as the sources of social ills" (p. 14).

Certainly, immigrants' dependent economic, legal, cultural, and social positions make them a target of varied forms of violence. Lovelace (1928/2002) in an introduction to *The Malleus Malleficarum (The Witches Hammer)*, noted that Jews and other foreigners, in addition to women who refused happy housewife roles, midwives, poets, gypsies, and people with disabilities counted among between 600,000 and 9 million people believed to have been publically tortured and brutally killed as witches in Europe in the span of 250 years of European Inquisitions. Certainly the Holocaust and the murder of over 6 million Jews based on scientific eugenic policies promoted by German Nazi government is another reminder of xenophobic and racist cruelty (Kuhl, 2002; Weikart, 2004). During the early part of twentieth century in the United States and the U.K. Jews and Slavs, fleeing persecutions, were barred immigrant entry, proclaimed feeble-minded and evolutionary unfit (Black, 2003; Tucker, 1996). Today immigrants are dying while crossing the borders seeking asylum and safety; they are targets of organized violence and crime; and they are denied legal and human rights just by virtue of their immigrant status (Cacho, 2000).

Xenophobic Violence and Brutality

Numerous recent reports show that in contemporary xenophobic societies treatment of immigrants is brutal and inhumane (Daley, 2016; UNHCR, 2018). As noted earlier, around the globe xenophobic violence is pronounced. According to the U.N. report on xenophobia in South Africa mistreatment of immigrants include varied forms of institutional and individual discrimination, stereotyping and verbal attacks, mistreatment by public and legal authorities, police and border patrol brutality, physical violence, and denial of access to economic and social benefits (Misago, Freemantle, & Landau, 2015). Kingdom of Bhutan is among the nations where inhumane and brutal treatment of Nepalese immigrant community is common, resulting in many abuses as well as their expulsion from Bhutan (Schultz, 2016). Elbagir, Razek, Platt, and Jones (2016) exposed horrific developments in Libya, where immigrants and refugees are sold as modern-day slaves. In the executive summary on immigration detention centers in the United States, Southern Poverty Law Center (2016) show that over 3 million undocumented immigrants who are detained "endure inhumane conditions in isolated facilities" while experiencing "aggressive" forms of enforcement by private prison corporations where detainees have no legal rights (online). At the time of writing this book, the United States has faced another moral crisis spurred by xenophobic policies and attitudes: forced separation of children from their parents at the border from migrants suspected of illegal crossing (Davis, 2018). Many European countries have experienced the rise of xenophobic far-right political and social groups in response to what is termed the European Refugee Crisis because by the end of 2016, over 5 million migrants and refugees from war-torn Syria, Iraq and Afghanistan have fled to Europe (UNHCR 2018). Studies on immigrant mental health and adjustment routinely show that immigrants suffer and struggle while they are simultaneously silenced (e.g., "aren't you glad you are here") and denied access to services (Berger, 2005; Hovey, 2000; Hovey & Magana, 2003; Yakushko, 2009b, 2010a, 2010b; Yakushko & Blodgett, 2018; Yakushko & Morgan-Consoli, 2014; Yakushko & Rajan, 2013). Lastly, migrants or people seeking to migrate worldwide are among the most vulnerable groups for human trafficking (i.e., termed new slavery), whether for sexual or labor exploitation, because of xenophobic perception that immigrants are sub-humans who can be exploited (Bales & Soodalter, 2010; Gozdziak & Collett, 2005; Shelley, 2010; Yakushko, 2009a).

Xenophobia, like other forms of prejudice and social oppression, is profoundly violent. However, unlike several other forms of socially discriminatory human behavior and attitudes (usually racism, anti-Semitism), many theorists have offered justifications of xenophobia as biological (evolutionary), universal, and unalterable. In contrast, theorists and social critics have elucidated how xenophobia develops, functions, and changes based on sociohistorical and psychological factors.

References

Addison, T., & Worswick, C. (2002). The impact of immigration on the earnings of natives: Evidence from Australian micro data. *Economic Record, 78*(240), 68–78.

Ahmed, S. (2013). *Strange encounters: Embodied others in post-coloniality.* London, UK: Routledge.

American Immigration Council. (2013). *The economic blame game: Immigration and unemployment.* Washington, DC: Immigration Policy Center. Retrieved June 2018, from https://www.americanimmigrationcouncil.org/sites/default/files/research/economic_blame_game.pdf.

Ana, O. S. (1999). 'Like an animal I was treated': Anti-immigrant metaphor in US public discourse. *Discourse and Society, 10*(2), 191–224.

Aruga, T. (1994). Reflections on the history of US-Japanese relations. *American Studies International, 32*(1), 8–16.

Bales, K., & Soodalter, R. (2010). *The slave next door: Human trafficking and slavery in America today.* Berkeley, CA: University of California Press.

Baldwin, J. (1993). *Nobody knows my name: More notes of a native son.* New York, NY: Vintage.

Bashford, A., & Levine, P. (Eds.). (2010). *The Oxford handbook of the history of eugenics.* New York: Oxford University Press.

Bauder, H. (2003). "Brain abuse", or the devaluation of immigrant labour in Canada. *Antipode, 35*(4), 699–717.

Berger, R. (2005). *Immigrant women tell their stories.* New York: The Haworth Press.

Black, E. (2003). *War against the weak: Eugenics and America's campaign to create a master race.* New York, NY: Four Walls Eight Windows.

Bosma, U. (2007). Beyond the Atlantic: Connecting migration and world history in the age of imperialism, 1840–1940. *International Review of Social History, 52*(1), 116–123.

Brigham, C. C. (1923). *A study of American intelligence.* Princeton, NJ: Princeton University Press.

Cacho, L. M. (2000). 'The people of California are suffering': The ideology of white injury in discourses of immigration. *Journal for Cultural Research, 4*(4), 389–418.

Californians for Population Stabilization. (2018). https://www.capsweb.org/.
Carballo, D. M., Roscoe, P., & Feinman, G. M. (2014). Cooperation and collective action in the cultural evolution of complex societies. *Journal of Archaeological Method and Theory, 21*(1), 98–133.
Casey, E. S., & Watkins, M. (2014). *Up against the wall: Re-imagining the US-Mexico border.* Austin, TX: University of Texas Press.
Chavez, L. R. (2001). *Covering immigration: Popular images and the politics of the nation.* Berkeley: University of California Press.
Cogdell, C. (2010). *Eugenic design: Streamlining America in the 1930s.* Philadelphia, PA: University of Pennsylvania Press.
Connelly, M. (2006, April 14). In polls, illegal immigrants are called burden. *New York Times*, p. A16.
Currell, S., & Cogdell, C. (Eds.). (2006). *Popular eugenics: National efficiency and American mass culture in the 1930s.* Athens, OH: Ohio University Press.
Curtin, P. (1984). *Cross-cultural trade in world history.* Cambridge: Cambridge University Press.
Daley, J. (2016, November 29). Why xenophobia is Dictionary.com word of the year. *Smithsonian Smart News.* Retrieved from https://www.smithsonianmag.com/smart-news/why-xenophobia-dictionarycoms-word-year-180961225/.
Danieli, Y. (1984). Psychotherapist's participation in the conspiracy of silence about the Holocaust. *Psychoanalytic Psychology, 1*(1), 23.
Danieli, Y. (1985). The treatment and prevention of long-term effects and intergenerational transmission of victimization: A lesson from Holocaust survivors and their children. *Trauma and its Wake, 1,* 295–313.
Daniels, R. (1977). *The politics of prejudice: The anti-Japanese movement in California and the struggle for Japanese exclusion.* Berkeley, CA: University of California Press.
Darwin, C. (1859). *On the origin of species: Or, the preservation of favoured races in the struggle for life.* London: Down, Bromley, Kent.
Darwin, C. (1888). *The descent of man and selection in relation to sex.* London: Murray.
Darwin, C. (1898). *The life and letters of Charles Darwin, including an autobiographical chapter* (Rev. ed., F. Darwin, Ed.). London, UK: John Murray.
Davenport, C. B. (1910). *Eugenics: The science of human improvement by better breeding.* New York: H. Holt.
Davis, J. H. (2018, June 15). Separated at the border from their parents: In six weeks, 1,995 children. *New York Times.* Retrieved from https://www.nytimes.com/2018/06/15/us/politics/trump-immigration-separation-border.html.
Dodson, B. (2010). Locating xenophobia: Debate, discourse, and everyday experience in Cape Town, South Africa. *Africa Today, 56*(3), 2–22.
Du Bois, W. E. B. (1903). *The talented tenth.* New York, NY: James Pott and Company.

Duggan, L. (2012). *The twilight of equality?: Neoliberalism, cultural politics, and the attack on democracy*. Boston, MA: Beacon Press.
Elbagir, N., Razek, R., Platt, A., & Jones, B. (2016). People for sale. Exclusive report, *CNN*. Retrieved June 18, 2018, from https://edition.cnn.com/2017/11/14/africa/libya-migrant-auctions/index.html.
Ervin, N. (1994). Immigration and the environment. In N. Mills (Ed.), *Arguing immigration: Are new immigrants a wealth of diversity… or a crushing burden?* (pp. 90–96). New York: Simon & Schuster.
Evans, W. S. (1931). *Organized eugenics*. New Haven, CT: American Eugenics Society.
Fanon, F. (1959/2008). *Black skin/White masks*. New York: Grove Press.
Frosh, S. (2004). Freud, psychoanalysis and anti-semitism. *Psychoanalytic Review, 91*(3), 309–330. https://doi.org/10.1521/prev.91.3.309.38302.
Gabaccia, D. R. (2002). *Immigration and American diversity: A concise introduction*. Malden, MA: Blackwell.
Galton, F. (1865). Hereditary talent and character. *Macmillan's Magazine, 12*(157), 318–327.
Galton, F. (1869). *Hereditary genius: An inquiry into its laws and consequences*. New York: Macmillan.
Galton, F. (1883). *Inquiries into the human faculty & its development*. London: J.M. Dent.
Galton, F. (1904). Eugenics: Its definition, scope, and aims. *American Journal of Sociology, 10*(1), 1–25.
Gambino, C. P., Acosta, Y. D., & Grieco, E. M. (2014). *English-speaking ability of the foreign-born population in the United States: 2012*. American Community Service Reports, ACS-26. Washington, DC: U.S. Census Bureau.
Gellner, E. (1995). Nationalism and xenophobia. In B. Baumgartl & A. Favell (Eds.), *New xenophobia in Europe* (pp. 6–9). London: Kluwer Law International.
Gibson, R. K. (2002). *The growth of anti-immigrant parties in Western Europe*. Lewiston, NY: Edwin Mellen Press.
Goddard, H. H. (1911). The elimination of feeble-mindedness. *The Annals of the American Academy of Political and Social Science, 37*(2), 261–272.
Goddard, H. H. (1912). *The Kallikak family: A study in the heredity of feeble-mindedness*. New York: Macmillan.
Goddard, H. H. (1914). *Feeble-mindedness*. New York: Macmillan.
Goddard, H. H. (1917). Mental tests and the immigrant. *Journal of Delinquency, 2*, 243–277.
Goss, S., Wade, A., Skirvin, J. P., Morris, M., Bye, K. M., & Huston, D. (2013). *Effects of unauthorized immigration on the actuarial status of the social*

security trust funds. Actuarial Note, 151. Baltimore, MD: Social Security Administration.

Gozdziak, E. M., & Collett, E. A. (2005). Research on human trafficking in North America: A review of literature. *International Migration, 43*(1–2), 99–128.

Grant, M. (1921). *The passing of the great race*. New York, NY: C. Scribner's Sons.

Hall, G. S. (1903). The white man's burden versus indigenous development of the lower races. *The Journal of Education, 58*(4, 1438), 83.

Hall, G. S. (1909). Evolution and psychology. In E. B. Poulton & G. S. Hall (Eds.), *Fifty years of Darwinism: Modern aspects of evolution* (pp. 251–267). Boston: H. Holt.

Hall, G. S. (1917a). *Jesus, the Christ, in the light of psychology*. New York: Doubleday, Page.

Hall, G. S. (1917b). Practical relations between psychology and the war. *Journal of Applied Psychology, 1*(1), 9–16. http://dx.doi.org/10.1037/h0070238.

Haynes, S. (2000). *Etruscan civilization: A cultural history*. Los Angeles, CA: Getty Publications.

Head, K., & Ries, J. (1998). Immigration and trade creation: Econometric evidence from Canada. *Canadian Journal of Economics, 31*(1), 47–62.

Hovey, J. D. (2000). Acculturative stress, depression, and suicidal ideation in Mexican immigrants. *Cultural Diversity and Ethnic Minority Psychology, 6*, 134–151.

Hovey, J. D., & Magana, C. J. (2003). Psychosocial predictors of anxiety among immigrant Mexican migrant farmworkers: Implications for prevention and treatment. *Cultural Diversity and Ethnic Minority Psychology, 8*, 274–289.

Johnson, G. E. (1980). The labor market effects of immigration. *Illinois Law Review, 33*(3), 331–341.

Jung, Y. (2004). Can Japan become a "society attractive to immigrants?": Identity, gender, and nation-states under globalization in East Asia. *International Journal of Japanese Sociology, 13*, 53–68.

Kivisto, P., & Faist, T. (2009). *Beyond a border: The causes and consequences of contemporary immigration*. London, UK: Sage.

Kuhl, S. (2002). *The Nazi connection: Eugenics, American racism, and German national socialism*. New York: Oxford University Press.

Lazarus, E. (1883). The new colossus. *A Century of Immigration, 1820–1924*. Library of Congress. Retrieved from https://memory.loc.gov/ammem/awhhtml/awlaw3/immigration.html.

Lee, M. T., & Martinez, R. (2009). Immigration reduces crime: An emerging scholarly consensus. In *Immigration, crime and justice* (pp. 3–16). Bingley, UK: Emerald Group Publishing Limited.

Leonhardt, D. (2007). Truth, fiction, and Lou Dobbs. *The New York Times.* Retrieved November 2, 2018 from https://www.nytimes.com/2007/05/30/business/30leonhardt.html.

Licata, L., & Klein, O. (2002). Does European citizenship breed xenophobia?: European identification as a predictor of intolerance towards immigrants. *Journal of Community and Applied Social Psychology, 12,* 323–337.

Linthicum, K. (2015). *Group says California immigration policies contribute to drought.* http://www.latimes.com/local/california/la-me-immigration-drought-20150524-story.html.

Lombardo, P. A. (Ed.). (2011). *A century of eugenics in America: From the Indiana experiment to the human genome era.* Bloomington, IN: Indiana University Press.

Lopez, G., & Radford, J. (2017). *Facts on U.S. immigrants, 2015.* Pew Research Center Reports. Retrieved June 18, 2018, from http://www.pewhispanic.org/2017/05/03/facts-on-u-s-immigrants/#2013-fb-authorized-pie.

Lovelace, W. (1928/2002). *Introduction to Malleus Maleficarum.* Online HTML Scripting Copyright © 1998–2001 by the Windhaven Network, Inc.

Lynn, R. (2001). *Eugenics: A reassessment.* New York: Praeger.

Lyons, P. D., & Clark, J. J. (2008). Interaction, enculturation, social distance, and ancient ethnic identities. In L. D. Webster, M. E. McBrinn, & E. Gamboa Carrera (Eds.), *Archaeology without borders: Contact, commerce, and change in the US Southwest and Northwestern Mexico* (pp. 185–207). Boulder: University Press of Colorado.

McClintock, A. (1995). *Imperial leather: Race, gender and sexuality in the colonial contest.* New York: Routledge.

McDougall, W. (1921). *National welfare and national decay.* London: Methuen & Co. Ltd.

Memmi, A. (2013). *The colonizer and the colonized.* New York: Routledge.

Merskin, D. L. (2011). *Media, minorities, and meaning: A critical introduction.* New York: Peter Lang.

Misago, J. P., Freemantle, I., & Landau, L. B. (2015). *Protection from xenophobia: An evaluation of UNHCR's regional office for Southern Africa's xenophobia related programmes.* Witwatersrand, South Africa: The African Center for Migration and Society. Retrieved from http://www.unhcr.org/55cb153f9.pdf.

Nowrasteh, A. (2016). *Terrorism and immigration: Risk analysis.* The CATO Institute, Policy Analysis No. 798. Retrieved June 18, 2018, from https://www.cato.org/publications/policy-analysis/terrorism-immigration-risk-analysis.

Oakley, R. (1996). *Tackling racist and xenophobic violence in Europe: Review and practical guidelines.* Strasbourg, Germany: Council of Europe Publishing.

Ortega, F., & Peri, G. (2009). *The causes and effects of international migrations: Evidence from OECD countries 1980–2005* (No. W14833). National Bureau of Economic Research.

Ousey, G. C., & Kubrin, C. E. (2009). Exploring the connection between immigration and violent crime rates in U.S. cities, 1980–2000. *Social Problems, 56*(3), 447–473.

Pearson, K. (1905). *National life from the standpoint of science.* London: Adam and Black.

Pearson, K. (1911). *The scope and importance to the state of the science of national eugenics.* London: Dulau and Company.

Pearson, K. (1930). *The life, letters and labours of Francis Galton.* Cambridge, UK: Cambridge University Press.

Perea, J. F. (1997). Introduction. In J. F. Perea (Ed.), *Immigrants out! The new nativism and the anti-immigrant impulse in the United States* (pp. 1–12). New York: New York University Press.

Pettigrew, T. F. (1998). Reactions toward the new minorities of Western Europe. *Annual Review of Sociology, 24,* 77–103.

Popenoe, P., & Johnson, R. H. (1918/1935). *Applied eugenics.* New York: Macmillan.

Pritzker, B. (2000). *A native American encyclopedia: History, culture, and peoples.* New York, NY: Oxford University Press.

Roosevelt, T. (1894, April). True Americanism. *The Forum Magazine*, p. 3.

Said, E. (1993). The politics of knowledge. In C. McCarthy & W. Crichlow (Eds.), *Race, identify and representation in education* (pp. 306–314). New York: Routledge.

Saleeby, C. W. (1911). *Woman and womanhood: A search for principles.* New York: Kennerley.

Sanger, M. (1919, February). Birth control and racial betterment. *Eugenical News.*.

Sanger, M. (1921). The eugenic value of birth control propaganda. *Birth Control Review, 5*(10), 1–10.

Schultz, E. (2016). Bhutanese refugee crisis: A brief history. *The Seattle Times.* Retrieved from https://www.seattletimes.com/seattle-news/bhutanese-refugee-crisis-a-brief-history/.

Selden, S. (1999). *Inheriting shame: The story of eugenics and racism in America.* New York: Teachers College Press.

Shelley, L. (2010). *Human trafficking: A global perspective.* Cambridge, UK: Cambridge University Press.

Shiochet, C. E. (2015). Immigrants and crime: Crunching the numbers. *CNN Reports.* Retrieved June 18, 2018, from https://www.cnn.com/2015/07/08/politics/immigrants-crime/.

Sloan, T. (2005). Globalization, poverty, and social justice. In G. Nelson & I. Prilleltensky (Eds.), *Community psychology: In pursuit of liberation and well-being* (pp. 309–329). New York: Palgrave.

Smith, J. D. (1985). *Minds made feeble: The myth and legacy of the Kallikaks.* Rockville, MD: Aspen.

Solnit, R. (2004). The Siege of the Sierra Club anti-immigration ideologues must not be allowed to hijack John Muir's vision. *Mother Jones*. Retrieved from https://www.motherjones.com/environment/2004/03/siege-sierra-club/.

Stein, G. J. (2002). From passive periphery to active agents: Emerging perspectives in the archaeology of interregional interaction. *American Anthropologist, 104*(3), 903–916.

Tactaquin, C. (1998). The greening of the anti-immigrant agenda. *Network News*, Spring Issue.

Taras, R. (2012). *Xenophobia and Islamophobia in Europe*. Edinburgh, UK: Edinburgh University Press.

Teaching Tolerance. (2011). *Ten myths about immigration*. Issues 39. Retrieved June 25, 2018, from https://www.tolerance.org/magazine/spring-2011/ten-myths-about-immigration.

Terman, L. M. (1916). *The measurement of intelligence*. New York: Houghton Mifflin.

Tucker, W. H. (1996). *The science and politics of racial research*. Urbana-Champaign: University of Illinois Press.

Unger, R. K., & Crawford, M. E. (1992). *Women and gender: A feminist psychology*. Philadelphia: Temple University Press.

UNHCR. (2018). *Refugee crisis in Europe*. Office of Emergencies, the United Nations. Retrieved from https://www.unrefugees.org/emergencies/refugee-crisis-in-europe/.

Vale, P. (2002). Migration, xenophobia, and security-making in post-apartheid South Africa. *Politikon, 29*, 7–29.

Weikart, R. (2004). *From Darwin to Hitler: Evolutionary ethics, eugenics, and racism in Germany*. New York: Palgrave Macmillan.

Wiggam, A. E. (1923). *The new decalogue of science*. Indianapolis, IN: Bobbs-Merrill.

Williamson, J. (1997). Globalization and inequality, past and present. *The World Bank Research Observer, 12*, 117–135.

Wistrich, R. S. (2011). *Demonizing the other: Antisemitism, racism and xenophobia*. London, UK: Routledge.

Yakushko, O. (2009a). Human trafficking: A review for mental health professionals. *International Journal for the Advancement of Counselling, 31*, 158–167. https://doi.org/10.1007/s10447-009-9075-3.

Yakushko, O. (2009b). Xenophobia: Understanding the roots and consequences of negative attitudes towards immigrants. *The Counseling Psychologist, 37*, 36–66.

Yakushko, O. (2010a). Stress and coping strategies in the lives of recent immigrants: A grounded theory model. *International Journal for the Advancement of Counselling, 32(4)*, 256–273.

Yakushko, O. (2010b). Working through interpreters with limited-English proficiency clients: A phenomenological investigation. *Professional Psychology: Research, Theory, and Practice, 41*(5), 449–455.

Yakushko. O. (2018a). Don't worry, be happy: Erasure of racism, sexism, and poverty in positive psychology. *Psychotherapy and Politics International, 16*, e1433.

Yakushko, O. (2018b). Witches, charlatans and old-wives tales: Critical history of women's indigenous knowledge in psychology. *Women and Therapy, 41*, 18–29.

Yakushko, O., & Blodgett, E. (2018). Counseling recent immigrants. In CC. Lee (Ed.), *Multicultural issues in counseling: New approaches to diversity* (pp. 215–227). Alexandria, VA: American Counseling Association.

Yakushko, O., & Morgan-Consoli, M. L. (2014). Politics and research of immigration: Implications for counseling and psychological scholarship and action. *Journal of Social Action in Counseling and Psychology, 6*, 98–122.

Yakushko, O., & Rajan, I. (2013). Refugees. In *The multicultural psychology case studies*. Thousand Oaks, CA: Sage (with student).

Yerkes, R. M. (1923). Eugenic bearing of measurements of intelligence. *The Eugenics Review, 14*(4), 225–229.

Yuval, I. J. (2011). Jews and Christians in the middle ages: Shared myths, common language. In R. S. Wistrich (Ed.), *Demonizing the other: Antisemitism, racism and xenophobia* (pp. 88–107). London: Routledge.

Zinn, H. (2010). *The twentieth century: A people's history*. New York: Harper & Row.

CHAPTER 4

Germs, Peacocks, and Scheming Domestics: Theories That Construct or Confront Xenophobia

Abstract Varied theories have been used to justify as well as critique xenophobia in social sciences. Evolutionary theories, just as during era of social Darwinism and eugenics, have been used to justify anti-immigrant sentiments as based on genetic differences and mythologized historical accounts. In addition, treating immigration as a "real" threat or focusing on immigrants' "acculturation" to dominant culture have also been central to creation of other theories of xenophobia. In contrast, many theorists have offered critical perspectives in regard to attitudes toward Others, foreigners, strangers, and minorities. Theories of guilt, splitting/projection, Motherland/Fatherland discourse, archetypes/hostile imagination, Other/Othering, social death, self-idealization/psychophobia, and de-colonialism are discussed in relation to xenophobia.

Keywords Evolutionary theories · Threat theories · Psychoanalytic theories · Decolonial theories

Constructing Xenophobia Through Biologized and Universalized Evolutionary Theories

Several theories explaining xenophobia offer an open justification of anti-immigrant prejudice as supposedly based on biological and social facts that accurately reflect reality. Among more vocal and publicized theoretical notions are those that draw, once again, on Darwinism,

O. Yakushko, *Modern-Day Xenophobia*,
https://doi.org/10.1007/978-3-030-00644-0_4

offering biological justifications of xenophobia as universal and invariable. Notably, evolutionary psychology is the re-branded field of scientific eugenics after having been re-titled for a short while "social biology" (both name changes came after being exposed in regard to their racist and sexist scholarship) (Bashford & Levine, 2010; Gur-Arie, 2014; Social Biology, 1973; Yakushko, in review). Critical social scholars have shown that evolutionary psychology that is based on social Darwinism continues to draw on falsely generalized and purposefully misrepresented accounts of animal and human groups (McKinnon, 2005; Ruti, 2015). These fictionalized accounts intentionally disregard tremendous social diversity among both animals and humans: the most intelligent, longest surviving or closest biologically to human species (e.g., whales, elephants, bees, the bonobos) are matriarchal and cooperative rather than patriarchal and violent (Fausto-Sterling, 1993; McKinnon, 2005; McKinnon & Silverman, 2005; Ruti, 2015). For example, according to Sarkar, "the African elephant (Loxodonta Africana) may have one of the most advanced of all mammalian social systems… along with unusually long lifespans and broadly overlapping generations, elephants have developed a complex matriarchal society" (p. 50).

In addition, evolutionary theories are grounded in the so-called cavemen or Pleistocene era, which is presented as based on viciousness, patriarchy, and dislike of any dissimilarity and thus, is typically used to justify both racist and sexist prejudice, violence, and discrimination (Bouchard, 1996; Buss, 1994, 2016; Lynn, 2001; Pinker, 2002; Rushton, 1995). For example, evolutionary psychologists include references to "ancestral women," whose exclusive role during the Pleistocene times was supposedly to defer to any male's sexual desire, and whose ancient evolutionary legacy apparently genetically imprinted women to expect "beatings, food depravation, diseases, abuse of children, and abandonment" (Buss, 2016, p. 47). In addition, same Pleistocene differences are used to scientifically explain supposed biological genetic differences in intelligence, aggression, sexual proclivities, and other forms of human differences as based on race as originating from Northern cold struggles to survive or Southern easy climate (Bouchard, 1996; Pinker, 2002; Rushton, 1995).

These evolutionary theoretical suppositions do not only have dubious empirical foundations, which are routinely used by both eugenic scientists and evolutionary psychologists to biologize and universalize sexism and racism as well as xenophobia, but also have been disproven by actual archeological accounts of ancient human cultures (Deloria, 1997).

For example, Seely (2012) in his book *Born Expecting the Pleistocene: Psychology and the Problem of Civilization* noted that definitive scientific evidence suggests that individuals living in the Pleistocene era did not face these forms of violence and were "relatively more egalitarian [than many contemporary cultures] –both in terms of gender equity and the lack of power-based class distinctions" (p. 63). Cross-cultural marriages, trade, and cooperation also were normative over millennia of human history: the ancient history of the Americas has been described as primarily "interactionist" and "enculturationist" (Lyons & Clark, 2008, p. 185).

Nevertheless, just like the original Darwinism, social Darwinism, and eugenics who justified racism, anti-Semitism, sexism, and colonialism on the grounds of supposedly scientific observations of animals as well as numerous large-scale statistical studies on humans (Bashford & Levine, 2010; Lombardo, 2011; Tucker, 1996), contemporary evolutionary psychologists, and academic eugenics supporters continue to uphold these theories to support varied forms of prejudice, including xenophobia. These contemporary social Darwinist scholars continue to advocate for explanations of human differences as based on genetics, hereditary, or biological (Bouchard, 1996; Gottfredson, 2005, 2012; Lynn, 2001; Pinker, 2002, 2018; Rushton, 1999; Rushton & Jensen, 2005). Not surprisingly, contemporary racist organizations, such as the infamous Pioneer Fund (2013), singles out funding for scientists who develop and produce sciences that justify human differences in terms of biology and evolutionary differences (Southern Poverty Law Center, 2017; Tucker, 1996; Yakushko, in review).

Specifically, evolutionary theories are frequently evoked to provide biological and genetically based explanations of xenophobia, such as the theory of Genetic Similarity (Rushton, 1990, 1995, 1999, 2005; van den Berghe, 1999) and other behavioral genetic and sociobiological theories (Reynolds & Vine, 1987). Rushton, who has been named among the most prolific racist scientists of the past half century, routinely used evolutionary explanations that belied supposed racial and national differences, including through measurement of intelligence, brain sizes, and genitalia sizes. His most notable work, the *Race, Evolution and Behavior* proclaimed that Black people's intelligence was limited by their smaller brain sizes and inversely larger genitalia, breasts, and buttocks (Rushton, 1995). In his speech to the *American Renaissance* conference, named among one of the most notable White Supremacy gatherings in the United States (A Convocation of Bigots:

The 1998 American Renaissance Conference, 1998), Rushton (2000) proclaimed "Whites have, on average, more neurons and cranial size than blacks... Blacks have an advantage in sport because they have narrower hips — but they have narrower hips because they have smaller brains." Moreover, Southern Poverty Law Center (2018), a group that maintains documentation of hate groups, noted about Rushton:

> Since 2002, Rushton has been president of the Pioneer Fund, which has for decades funded dubious studies linking race to characteristics like criminality, sexuality and intelligence. Pioneer has long promoted eugenics, or the "science" of creating "better" humans through selective breeding [eugenics]. Set up in 1937 and headed by Nazi sympathizers, the group strove to "improve the character of the American people" through eugenics and procreation by people of white colonial stock. Pioneer has financed a number of leading race scientists, lavishing large sums each year on those who work to "prove" inherent racial differences that the vast majority of scientists regard as nonsense. (online)

Thus, Rushton's (2005) explanation of xenophobia, like other forms of prejudice toward out-groups, was termed the Genetic Similarity Theory, based on the evolutionary Kinship theory, which was apparently developed to

> explain ethnic nepotism and people's need to identify and be with their 'own kind' (Rushton et al. 1984 and 1986; Rushton 1989a, 1995, 2004; Rushton and Bons 2005). Nationalists often claim that their nation has organic continuity and 'ties of blood' that make them 'special' and different from outsiders, a view not fully explained by ethno-symbolism. Although the term 'ethnicity' is recent, the sense of kinship, group solidarity and common culture to which it refers is often as old as the historical record (Hutchinson and Smith 1996). Genetic Similarity Theory extends Smith's theory and the unity of knowledge by providing the next link, the necessary biological mooring. (p. 490)

Rather than acknowledging the influence of social norms and social values in creating in-group and out-group ideologies, including in regard to treatment of race, nationality, gender and more, Rushton proposes that children and adults are genetically predisposed to treat those they perceive similar to them with liking while disliking those they perceive dissimilar to them:

> Even very young children typically show a clear preference for others of their own ethnic heritage (Aboud 1988). In fact, the process of making racial groupings has been shown to result from a natural tendency to classify people into 'kinds'. Children quickly begin to sort people into 'basic kinds' by sex, age, size and occupation. Experiments show that at an early age children clearly expect race to run in families (Hirschfield 1996). Very early in life, a child knows which race it belongs to, and which ones it doesn't. (p. 500)

Other evolutionary scholars proposed similar theories (Dawkins, 1981; MacDonald, 2005; Pinker, 2002; Rushton, 2005; van der Dennen, 1987; Wilson, 1975). Moreover, intelligence as evidence of evolutionary superiority, which has been central to Darwinism, social Darwinism, and eugenics (Bouchard, 1996; Brigham, 1923; Buss, 2009; Darwin, 1859; 1898; Galton, 1865, 1869, 1883; Goddard, 1911, 1919; Gottfredson, 2005, 2012; Hall, 1903, 1909; Lynn, 2001; Pearson, 1905, 1911; Pinker, 2002, 2005, 2018; Rushton & Jensen, 2005; Wilson, 1975; Yerkes, 1923) continues to focus on supposedly hereditary or genetic differences in intelligence that underlie hatred toward immigrants. Whereas this book briefly highlighted examples of xenophobic rhetoric reproduced in scientific studies during the first part of the twentieth century, recent "scholarship" continues to focus on genetic intelligence deficiencies of immigrants. In the United States this new difference is emphasized for the Latino immigrants, with studies claiming that Latinos possess low levels of intelligence that will supposedly cause U.S. billions if not trillions of dollars if immigration reforms with a focus on integrating Latino immigrants take place (Hatewatch, 2013). Richwine, who conducted this study and proclaimed this Latino-White intelligence differences, based his research on evolutionary psychology writings by Rushton and other scholars (Bouie, 2013). According to Bouie's (2013) report, Richwine's dissertation study promoted by anti-immigrant, White Supremacy, and nativists groups, stated that "No one knows whether Hispanics will ever reach IQ parity with whites, but the prediction that new Hispanic immigrants will have low-IQ children and grandchildren is difficult to argue against" (online). Bouie further highlighted that, just like the eugenicists of the early twentieth century, Richwine argued "the relative IQs of immigrant groups should be weighed when determining who receives permanent entry into the United States" (online).

What is not discussed is the fact that so-called genetic similarity across national borders is an unqualified fiction considering the tremendous ethnic diversity of most world cultures today, especially the countries where xenophobia is most manifest. In addition, according to scholars, humanity shares 99.9% genetic similarity (National Genome Research Institute, 2006)—such enormous level of similarity should produce a feeling of "genetic similarity" for all groups rather than producing a feeling of such profound difference as to merit ethnic conflict and anti-immigrant prejudice. In addition, Darwinist and eugenicists emphasis on intelligence as defined and measured through Western (and eugenicists in origin) methods and concepts, has been debunked by many psychologists and scientists, yet it persists as a definitive measure of evolutionary "fitness" in racist Darwinism-influence sciences (Gould, 1995; Tucker, 1996; Yakushko, in review).

Another evolutionary-based dislike is supposedly based on fear of germs or diseases that are perceived as being a threat to the health of native-born population by the foreigners (Falkner, Schaller, Park, & Duncan, 2004). This theory appears to hold limited, if any, explanatory power, since almost 90% of immigrants enter the country legally, and those who seek permanent status must undergo medical testing (U.S. Citizen and Immigration Services, 2018; Yakushko, 2009b). In addition, the very same foreign individuals perceived as especially dangerously diseased (i.e., undocumented immigrants) by the native-born, are the most likely to be employed by those same native-born in intimate domestic capacities, such as raising their children or cleaning/maintaining their homes, hotels, and businesses. More than a third of unauthorized immigrants in the United States are employed in service occupations while large proportions of others are involved in growing and food packaging agricultural work that places them in close contact with items consumed by the native-born (Pew Hispanic Center, 2016). Very similar biological explanations of minorities as diseased (i.e., having bad germo-plasms and special susceptibility to infectious diseases especially STDs and tuberculosis), were used to create "Whites only" bathrooms and water fountains, and segregate Jews and Roma people into ghettos and camps (Codgell, 2010; Currell & Cogdell, 2006; Kuhl, 2002; Merskin, 2011; Selden, 1999).

Echoing the other part of the Darwinist theory of differences (i.e., competition to survive among the fitness and procreation), another evolutionary explanation is focused on supposed lekking (e.g., akin to peacock tail-showing off) by native-born males who perceived foreign-born males as a threat in their exclusive access to female native-born for procreation (Kanazawa & Frerichs, 2001). In contrast, consider that native-born privileged Western males are among the most likely individuals to participate in international mail order bride businesses in pursuit of intimate partners, which has exploded in the past twenty years (U.S. Congress, 2004; Yakushko & Rajan, 2017). In fact, White Western middle age males who have been divorced, who have traditional (patriarchal) views of gender relations, who seek docile and dependent female partners, who ascribe to fundamentalist or conservative social views are among the most likely to seek female partners across the borders (Yakushko & Rajan, 2017). In addition, privileged Western males are the instigators and beneficiaries of human trafficking of women and girls (as well as boys) for sexual exploitation (Bales & Soodalter, 2010; Gozdziak & Collett, 2005; Shelley, 2010; Yakushko, 2009a). An argument that native-born men dislike the arrival of immigrants because of the threat to their procreative male prowess in fight over the females seems both essentially sexist as well as entirely false.

Constructing Xenophobia Through "Realistic" Threat Theories

Outside of evolutionary explanations, other theories of xenophobia similarly offer justifications of its supposed legitimacy (Fry, 2001; Rydgren, 2004; Stephan & Stephan, 1996). Rather than openly naming xenophobia as a form of social violence and social prejudice, scientists as well as members of the media often discuss such questions as "should the needs and rights of the host country or the needs and the rights of its migrants be seen as primary?", "are selective immigration policies discriminatory?", or a "crushing burden" (e.g., LeMay, 2004; Mills, 1994). Allegedly realistic concerns and fears of the host communities, which discriminate again the newcomers, are used by theorists as realistic causes (Fry, 2001; Rydgren, 2004). Economic fears, such as perception that immigrants cost jobs, social resources, and damage to the environment (Buck et al., 2003; Ervin, 1994; Ommundsen & Larsen, 1997; Ommundsen, Van der Veer, Yakushko, & Ullenberg, 2013; Tactaquin, 1998; Thornton & Mizuno, 1999; Van der Veer, Ommundsen, Yakushko, & Higler, 2011; Van der Veer et al., 2013; Yakushko, 2009b). These "reality" based concern were the same as racist and sexist concerns that greater inclusion of racial minorities and women was detrimental to the economy, cost jobs to White men, and resulted in high social costs (Runciman, 1966; Ott, 1995). As noted earlier, numerous studies and reports have found the common perceived threats of immigrants and migration to be not only based on myths, but in fact be the very opposite (e.g., immigrants do not take jobs of the native-born groups; greater number of immigrants in a given community reduces crime and violence).

Nevertheless, social theorists continue to exploit these myths in creation of their theories. One such theory, entitled Realistic Group Conflict theory (Sherif, Harvey, White, Hood, & Sherif, 1961) suggests that competition for access to the limited resources results in a struggle between the in-group (i.e., native-born) and the out-group (i.e., foreign-born). Competition for these purportedly limited resources between groups leads to prejudices against the out-group. Another similar theory, called the Integrated Theory of Prejudice (Stephan & Stephan, 1996; Stephan, Ybarra, & Bachman, 1999), suggested that because the in-group experiences a real threat to their economic and political power, their cultural values, their worldviews, which causes their anxiety to escalate, prejudice develops. Arguably, the scholars may be aware that these perceived threats are fictional and are created by the privileged community seeking to find threat and demonize a marginalized group. Ostensibly, Stephan and Stephan (2013) theorized that when individuals from the in-group perceive a supposed threat from the out-group, this conflict creates a challenge to their self-image, resulting in anxiety. They further hypothesized that when the in-group members interact with the out-group whom they stereotype to be violent, stupid, and indolent, they evidently feel uneasy about such interactions. In reading this scholarship, it is unclear whether the authors recognize that the so-called threats of the out-group (e.g., immigrant community) are imagined and are based on prejudicial biased views rather than realities. In fact, the supposed anxiety and worry of the in-group individuals is treated as somehow normative and understandable, rather than indicative of their prejudices and purposeful misinformation.

Confronting Xenophobia Through Social Group Theories

In contrast to theories that use genetic and biological explanations or who treat prejudices as realistic concerns, other theories focused on anti-immigrant attitudes as a form of socially violent prejudice, such as in the examinations of authoritarianism, social dominance, system justification and Just World beliefs. Theories related to right-wing authoritarianism were developed in the 1950s in efforts to explain fascism and other right-wing ideologies (Adorno, Frenkel-Brunswik, Levinson, & Sanford, 1950).

Altemeyer (1981, 1988) further expanded the study of right-wing authoritarian personality. According to Altemeyer, right wing authoritarianism was based on two processes: (1) splitting individuals into in-groups and out-groups, marked by hostility toward the out-groups as perception of them as a threat and (2) ascribing goodness, righteousness, morality, and other positive factors to one's own in-group while projecting the opposites into the out-group.

A more recent theory, Social Dominance Orientation, similarly focuses on development of prejudice as related to the need to create categories of those who belong and who do not belong. Pratto, Sidanius, Stallworth, and Malle (1994) have suggested that individuals with high social dominance orientation believe that social structures are inherently hierarchical and that such structures must be upheld (e.g., native-born individuals thus must be held in higher regard than foreigners). According to Pratto et al. "the extent to which one desires that one's in-group dominate and be superior to outgroups" (p. 742). Social dominance over others, according to these theories, requires views of outsiders or different others as inferior, and the denial of their rights typically take the form of indirect actions (i.e., rejection of affirmative action).

Another theoretical standpoints that challenged, rather than defended prejudice, was offered by Jost and Banaji (1994) in their System Justification theory, which emphasized that prejudice functions to maintain the status quo in the society (i.e., immigrants as dispossessed poor laborers). In their more recent review of their theory, Jost, Banaji, and Nosek (2004) highlighted that their theory can elucidate such processes as "ideological motive to justify the existing social order," "internalization of inferiority among members of disadvantaged groups," reasons for why prejudice operates primarily on the "implicit, nonconscious level of awareness" and reasons for why this prejudice about themselves is "paradoxically...strongest among those who are most harmed by the status quo" (p. 881).

Lastly, a related concept is the belief that the world is just, and that bad things happen to people who deserve them (e.g., wars, economic problems) whereas good people enjoy a good life because they earned and deserve such goodness (Lerner, 1980). According to Just World d Belief theorists Furnham (1992),

> One of the most robust findings in the literature is the fact that just world beliefs help people cope with disturbing or threatening events (rape, poverty, racism) and that the shared experience of these events causes people to develop a consensual view of reality. Because just world beliefs reduce or prevent feelings of guilt, they are retained and passed on to succeeding generations. In Third World countries, just world beliefs held by the rich and powerful condemn or devalue the poor. Some people believe in a just world because of their personal pathology and experiences (individual functionalism), but there is evidence that just world beliefs are a function not only of personal experience, but also of societal functionalism, (i.e., a country's structural and societal factors). (p. 327)

Confronting Xenophobia Through a Theory of Ethnocentric Guilt

Thus, another theory that may explain xenophobic attitudes as a form of prejudice that interacts and approximates racism could be termed Ethnocentric Guilt, related to guilt engendered by Just World Belief theory Furnham (1992). This concept draws on the theory of White Guilt, which was proposed by multiple social critics and scholars such as Frantz Fanon (1959/2008) and James Baldwin (1965). In his *Black Skin/White Masks* Fanon (1959/2008) notes that White colonizers focus on blackness as associated with violence, evil and sine, whereas they also perceive whiteness with goodness such as "the bright look of innocence, the white dove of piece, magical heavenly light" (p. 146). Baldwin (1998) discussed the "willed innocence" of whiteness, which can only be challenged when an individual acknowledges the history of oppression. In social scholarship, Steele (1990) suggested that in a racist society divide along Black-White lines, White individuals experience unconscious guilt because of their "ill-gotten" advantages as well as accompanied "inevitable gratitude one feels for being White rather than Black in America" (p. 499). This awareness of racism and its privileges for White individuals also results in increased defensiveness and denials of discrimination specifically in order to assuage feelings of guilt and shame (Allport, 1954; Ioanide, 2014; Layton, 2009, 2010; Tatum, 1994). In models of White racial identity development, the capacity to experience and deal with these feelings is one of the most important stages (Helms, 1990; Ioanide, 2014; Tatum, 1994).

Incapacity to tolerate guilt and shame as vital emotions for personal and collective change, both individuals and culture seek to flee into all-good feelings and reestablishment of innocence and goodness. According to Steele (1990) "guilt makes us afraid for ourselves, and thus generates as much self-preoccupation as concern for others. The nature of preoccupation is always the redemption of innocence, the reestablishment of good feeling about oneself" (p. 501). Thus, one of the institutional forms of White guilt can be found in social policies and cultural narratives, which emphasize not the equality but movements to assuage guilt through minor quick-fix solutions. When such solutions do not result in changes the dominant group desires, the blame is quickly assigned to the minority group, which is "unwilling to change," is ungrateful, is incapable of internal attributions and personally achieved happiness, and is, after all, responsible for their own problems. In addition, management of inequalities produces feelings of supposed injury among the racial majority individuals, resulting in such terms as "reverse discrimination," "white injury," and self-representation as being "color-blind" (Cacho, 2000; Ioanide, 2014; Layton, 2010; Lipsitz, 2006; Silva, 2003).

I propose the concept of Ethnocentric Guilt, which also certainly encompasses aspects of White guilt since xenophobia in Western countries is entangled in racism. This guilt draws on significant history of imperialism and colonialism, and more recently, history of oppressive globalized capitalism, which has taken a form of both economic and political forms of domination over other nations (Bosma, 2007; Williamson, 1997). As noted earlier, the greatest proportion of migrants to Europe are arriving from countries that were colonized and occupied by the very same European powers over the span of hundreds of years. In many cases, such as the occupation of Northern Africa by the French, were brutal (Fanon, 1959/2008). In the United States, in addition to contemporary history of clandestine political involvements, the relentless demand for drugs in the United States, and economic policies such as the North American Financial and Trade Agreement (NAFTA), which impoverished especially people of Mexico and Central America, prior history of violent take over of Southern American territories during the eighteenth-century war with Mexico are also at play (Casey & Watkins, 2014).

Recent declared and undeclared wars as well as destabilizing capitalist investments that ensued in profound social instabilities in Central America, Africa, many parts of Asia and the Middle East, have created horrific conditions that pushed millions of people to migrate for survival.

Whereas many privileged Western individuals feel humanitarian impulses and, if pressed, guilt and shame for their contribution to these global evils—recognizing the financial and social advantages from these exploitative and violent strategies, including their affordable goods (e.g., cheap clothing, technology, food items)—these feelings, like those of White guilt, appear to transform to defensive and angry reactions when facing immigrants. It is the immigrants rather than corporations that are vilified and punished. Cacho (2000) highlighted that the

> undocumented labor enables corporations to bypass labor and antidiscrimination laws as well as health and safety regulations because undocumented workers are made too vulnerable by immigration law to be able to utilize their rights as workers under state labor laws. (p. 22)

Still native-born people decry being over-run by hoards and tides of dangerous aliens; they blame said immigrants for all manner of social ills, including educational declines, environmental crises, and rise in crime. These perceptions and misconceptions are, as noted before, have no bearing in reality. Thus, it seems that guilt, in this case, the Ethnocentric Guilt, operates to both unconsciously acknowledge the realities and even causes of immigration while dehumanizing and vilifying immigrants themselves.

Such affective responses, as noted by those who write about White Guilt (Steele, 1990), when not corresponding to factual data or even acknowledged commitments to tolerance and social compassion, point to what Fanon (1959/2008) termed paralogical or prelogical reactions. Fanon wrote about violently degrading colonial rule of Europeans over the African nations in mid-twentieth century. He noted that factual evidence was eschewed while conscious and unconscious beliefs, desires, phobias, and fantasies of what constituted a Black Africa became the foreground for White individuals. Fanon highlighted that to term these reactions irrational was not accurate—in fact, the ideologies of twentieth-century colonialism were especially supported by numerous scientific data, based on social Darwinism and eugenics, that could be used to prop such views and ignore all other evidence. For example, Fanon pointed to the multiple "genetic" studies that supposedly proved that "negroes" possessed not only genes of "cannibalism," but also those that marked them as ideal for enslavement and hard labor—a "shameful science!" in Fanon's words (p. 187).

The affective responses of the colonizers and racists, Fanon argued, often sought and found rational explanations, which were readily available in larger social structures and norms, in cultural discourse and its ideologies, or in economic and material indicators (e.g., Africans as poor and illiterate). Similar conditions appear to operate in relation to the Ethnocentric Guilt. Whereas scholars have put out studies that contradict xenophobic fantasies and phobias, xenophobic groups and xenophobic scholars insist on representing immigrants and migration as dangerous while continually producing new sciences of, once again, perilously low intelligence and moral qualities of the newcomers (Bouie, 2013; Hatewatch, 2013).

Layton (2010) in her work on what she calls perverse modes of subjectivity highlighted that individuals and groups can elect to disavow truths of their experiences or observations and replace them with lies in order to protect themselves from a sense of personal responsibility for own and other's suffering. She argued that this personal responsibility is evoked by neoliberal or fundamentalist capitalist ideals, which in the West insist on idealized versions of individuals as autonomous, self-regulating, and self-sustaining. Echoing the assertions in regard to White guilt and Ethnocentric guilt, Layton stated that "the trauma of indifference to increasing economic inequality has indeed been registered but has been disavowed [split off, made unconscious]" (p. 309).

Confronting Xenophobia Through Theories of Splitting and Projection

The discourse of immigrants as a "refuse" from other countries can then also support the self-perception of being caring toward otherwise impoverished, criminal, uneducated, and dumb immigrant hordes. Splitting individuals, like splitting one's own human experiences into all good versus all bad, civilized versus primitive, autonomous and adult-like versus needy and child-like, is psychologically and socially common (Bollas, 2018; Freud, 1930, 1953). Such splitting also then necessitates a projection of those aspects of oneself or society, which are found to be unacceptable (i.e., badness, primitively, neediness), into others that are viewed as separate and different from oneself (Bollas, 2018; Frosh, 2004; Ioanide, 2014; Layton, 2010). In fact, Dalal (2002) proposed that it is not that different individuals and groups evoke a negative or problematic response from us because they are different but it is because within ourselves we contain unacceptable and unwanted impulses and emotions, which need to be discharged and found outside of oneself. Fanon (1959/2008) similarly discussed how mid-twentieth- century European struggles to accept their own aggression, sexual voraciousness, and dependency resulted in splitting off (i.e., Europeans are civilized, scientific, and pure) and projecting into colonized Africans (e.g., Africans as violent, sexually deviant, and servile).

Scholars like Bollas (2018) emphasized that many psychoanalytic theories were created in reaction to horrific European wars, marked by profound splitting and demonization of groups. He proposed that whereas "splitting (of the object or the self) is an ordinary mental action," this mental process of inclusivity of experiences, feelings, and inner states can result in "a vicious cycle," during which individuals as well as groups can "split off unwanted facts, especially if they are facts about our self" in order to maintain an idealized self-perceptions while at the same time giving ourselves "mental licensing" or permission "to ravage the [supposedly evil] world" (pp. 16–17). These processes, Bollas argued, often manifest themselves in collective or individual euphoria "by allowing us to float away from the more sober sides of reality" in order to create "a rosy pictures of the future, and projecting the unwanted parts of self and society into "the other"" (pp. 16–17).

Thus, one of the ways to dehumanize immigrants while maintaining a humanitarian perspective is to split them off from other human beings by presenting them pitiful and needy in contrast to one's own supposedly successful, happy, and independent ("great") nation. Such views can help the native-born community to sustain its self-perception of being open and kind ("give me your tired and poor") while at the very same time deporting, dehumanizing, condescending to, or criminalizing these same immigrants because they are a threat, including being needy and poor (i.e., taking one's own resources). It is notable that often humanitarian impulses toward immigrants are evoked through an emphasis on immigrant children, such as the DREAMers or children separated from their parents at the borders by immigrant authorities (Davis, 2018). The Europeans and the world were galvanized by the picture of drowned Syrian refugee boy Alan Kurdi (Ensor, 2016). Undoubtedly, mistreatment of vulnerable children reflects horrific social cruelty. However, reactions to children typically evoke paternalizing and condescending views (Merskin, 2011) whereas all immigrants, regardless of their age, should be treated with full human rights and dignity. As the father of Alan Kurdi stated, "photo of my dead son has changed nothing" (Ensor, 2016, online). As Layton (2010) noted, when individuals and groups deny their vulnerability and social needs, especially through seeking to differentiate life into superior and inferior aspects, "refuge has been increasingly south in the grandiose fantasy of superiority" and resentment in order to disassociate with others' suffering and needs (p. 309).

In fact, the needy child-like immigrants are likely to evoke conscious or unconscious feelings of resentment not only because the native-born individuals must struggle with guilt, shame, sense of responsibility, and sense of hopelessness, but the very same children evoke recognition of how many resources they will supposedly appropriate from native-born children. According to Cacho (2000), who wrote about media reactions in wake of California's Proposition 187, which served to deny services to undocumented immigrants, "ideology of white injury both conceals and sustains inequitable social relations" (p. 389). Layton (2010) further suggested that such reactions within the context of neoliberal societies that emphasize competition, survival, and autonomy, individuals from the dominant group may be left to oscillate between their sense of omnipotence and their profound sense of helplessness and uselessness.

Certainly, Jews throughout the last millennium of European history, were similarly perceived as a social and religious threat, projections in whom demonized them as supposedly wicked in contrast to pure and good Christians (Wistrich, 2011). Theories in regard to anti-Semitism are another vital source of understanding xenophobia. Among key contributions to the psychological foundations of this prejudice was the work of S. Freud, whose radical turn to acknowledging the unconscious and implicit influences on human behavior has served as the foreground for most critical theories of the past century (1964).

Freud, a Jewish man facing anti-Semitism and the rise of Nazism, offered several interpretations for hatred of the Jews. Indeed, one of his primary theories focused on guilt and unconscious aggression it generated "in the form of hostility against intruders" (Freud, 1930, p. 21). Christian notions of Father God sacrificing his divine Son with their implications for the unconscious, reflecting the individual unresolved murderous anger of sons toward their fathers, was displaced by projecting this violence into Jews, who were to blame for Christ's death (Freud, 1953). Another theory focused on the potential for sibling rivalry between Jews, the original God's chosen people, and the converted gentiles (Christians). Freud also wondered if Christian's unconscious battle with their religiously-driven superego was also directed away from oneself toward Jews, who were sinful and ungodly. Using the term "scapegoating," Freud (1930) in his *Civilization and its Discontents* discussed how focusing on reviling an out-group as carrying out social evils (i.e., sex, violence, greed) permitted the in-group to maintain its conscious illusions of their own goodness and purity. Lastly, because in Freud's time Jewish males were among the only groups to be circumcised, castration anxieties and sexual dread among the uncircumcised men could contribute to unconscious hatred of Jews as well as women who were perceived as a threat. In Freud's (1909) words, "the castration complex is the deepest unconscious root of anti-Semitism; for even in the nursery little boys hear that a Jew has something cut off his penis—a piece of his penis, they think—and this gives them a right to despise Jews" (p. 36).

Confronting Xenophobia in Relation to Motherland/Fatherland Discourse

Psychoanalytic theories in relation to xenophobic and other prejudicial reactions critiqued and extended Freud's theories (1930, 1953). Recently, an Oedipal or child/parent conflict as well as sibling rivalry configuration was extended to processes of immigration in that the imago of one's place of birth as a Home or as Motherland or Fatherland evokes fantasies and actions that cast an immigrant as caught between loyalties to one versus the other parent as well as in competition with new siblings (Zylinska, 2004). Central to psychoanalysis is the concept of overdetermination or recognition that no theory or explanation can fully elucidate complex human experiences (Freud, 1953). Thus, the Oedipal and sibling rivalry explanation may contribute to part of the determination of why the host community perceives the newcomers as intruders on their home and Motherland. Like in a Biblical allegory of the older "good" brother who is resentful of the return of his "prodigal" brother, seemingly limited resources and "love" from the Motherland or Fatherland. In addition, psychoanalytic scholars like Akhtar (2010) discussed unresolved Oedipal processes, common among traumatized individuals who often choose to migrate in search of survival and wholeness away from what is perceived as unloving and rebuffing "homeland," can also shape immigrants' experiences of belonging, rejection, self-silencing, dejection, or willingness to assert their personal or cultural agency.

Confronting Xenophobia Through Theories the Other and Otherizing

Another set of critical and psychoanalytically-grounded theories focus on experiences of being the Other and being Otherized. Concepts related to creation and promulgation of the Other focus on a difference and the distance created by a subject (i.e., individual, distinct group) from person or persons perceived as wholly different and non or anti-self. These theories draw on similar notions to splitting and projection although they also expand and differ from them.

Among the first to propose theory of the Other was Sartre (1943/1956), whose ideas in regard to creation of the Other also include development of the Gaze, which strips the Other of its autonomy, agency, identity and freedom of action (i.e., the Other as an object functions and exists only in relation to the gazing subject). Sartre further emphasized that the relations between the subject and the Other object are always antagonistically constellated along the axis of being dominated or dominating.

Levinas (1996) further contributed to theories of the Other but noted that the created difference evokes ethical responsibility for those perceived as different and opposite to oneself. Among the most common theories of the Other was offered by Lacan (1978/1998), who explicated varied modalities of otherness, including the symbolic Other which becomes the source of the unconscious speech and identity for the subject. In this theory, the immigrant and the foreigner is what creates and constitutes the identity of a nativist native-born person. Spivak (2013) extended the theory of the Other to concept of Othering. Her work emphasizes the desire for power and domination, the construction of hegemonic relations and discourse, as integral to the part of Othering of people on the margins. Thus, immigrants and migration are not only constructed but are legally constrained through presence or absence of their documents, their incapacity to vote or have legal representation (i.e., legal permanent residents of Green Card holders). Le Espiritu (2003) termed that groups such as immigrants are "differentially included"—they are deemed "integral to the nations' economy, culture identity, and power – but integral only or precisely because of their designated subordinate standing" (p. 56). Cacho (2000) noted how in discourse on immigration and race "human value is made intelligible through racialized, sexualized, spatialized, and state-sanctioned violence" (p. 4). Cacho further highlights the discourse that shapes this Otherizing when dominant representations of immigrants casts them as "illegal aliens," "gang members," and "terrorists." Another aspect of Otherizing involves fetishizing groups on the margins. Ahmed (2013) introduced the term "stranger fetishism," which employs an emphasis not on supposedly strange or unknown others but on determining these individuals or groups indeed to be the strangers. According to Ahmed, the stranger "assumes a life of its own only insofar as it is cut off from its histories of its determination" (p. xx).

The processes that underlie creation of the Other and Otherizing, are also central to an emphasis that the dominant/dominating, master/slave, good/bad, native/foreign are accepted and internalized by both in-group and the out-group. Writing about experiences of African American people, Du Bois (1903) proposed the term "double consciousness," which he described as a "sense of always looking at one's self through the eyes of others, of measuring one's soul by the tape of a world that looks on in amused contempt and pity" (p. XX). African psychoanalyst and critical scholar Fanon (1959/2008) focused on psychological and cultural alienation, especially unconscious self-alienation, that is produced by colonial practices and discourse. Compradors, a term Fanon uses for Black Africans who donned on White European masks through accepting the racist colonialist views and then further promoting these to other Blacks, were an outcome of such alienation. A contemporary evidence of such unconscious colonization that accepts and reproduces racist, sexist, and xenophobic views can be found in voting records: in recent presidential election in the United States, over 50% of women voted for a candidate who boasted of sexual violence and denigrated women; one-third of Latinos also voted for this candidate who has openly espoused racist rhetoric toward Latinos (Gomez, 2016). In fact, recent immigrants rarely appear to be visible agents in protests against violent, dehumanized forms of xenophobia they experience—it is the second generation of immigrants who are born to foreign-born immigrant parents that seem far more visible in both their resistance and distress (i.e., an alternative explanation to so-called Latino Paradox) (Perea, 1997).

Confronting Xenophobia Through Theories of Social Death

A theory that may further elucidate the absence of immigrant presence uses the term "social death" (Cacho, 2000; Patterson, 1982). Patterson (1982) suggested that although enslaved Africans were ostensibly physically alive, their lives which were stripped of all human, legal, and cultural rights, contributed to their experience of social death. Cacho's (2000) recent book entitled *Social Death: Racialized Rightlessness and the Criminalization of the Unprotected* discussed the criminalization of many immigrants, who are criminalized by being prevented from "being law-abiding" (p. 4), "deemed deserving of discipline and punishment but not worthy of protection" (p. 5). In her words, immigrants who are denied legal status "criminalized, demonized, and rendered rightless," making them "permanently criminalized people are the groups" who are "ineligible for personhood" (p. 6). Moreover, Cacho highlights the absurdity of human beings actually selecting their criminalized status, as if the

> "illegal" status is a choice made by rational individuals who are ultimately resigned to being underpaid, cheated, and abused because after "calculating" the risks or "gambling" against the odds, each person presumably decided that undocumented status would still be "worth" it. (p. 19)

The xenophobic rhetoric further announces that undocumented immigrants "should feel lucky to be exploited if they are paid at all" (p. 19). These forms of criminalization and dehumanization are, in Cacho's words, an evidence of social death imposed on immigrants, especially undocumented immigrants.

Post-, anti- and de-colonial scholars also offered theories that further expanded understanding of prejudice that is often organized around national and racial differences. Homi Bhabha (1990) in his contributions entitled *Nations and Narration* highlighted how groups operate by creating "imagined community," which insist on establishing a sense of historical continuity and illusory identity in order to control "international perspectives" and "founding fiction." These narratives, according to Bhabha, necessitate creation of discourse that requires the continual use of stereotypes and fetishisms. These stereotypes always cast people into split categories, either idealizing them (i.e., model minority) or demonizing them (i.e., criminals) while denying people their humanity, complexity, and hybrid or multiple identities.

Confronting Xenophobia Through Theories of Self-Idealization and Psychophobia

Among the most recognized contemporary psychoanalytic scholars, Christopher Bollas has offered multiple additional theories to help understand the social tendencies toward demonizing groups of supposedly "other" individuals while denying them full human rights. In his most recent book *Meaning and Melancholia: Life in the Age of Bewilderment*, Bollas (2018) highlighted search for idealized self and idealized group to belong to often have led to denial of complexities and multiplicities that define human experience while replacing them with rigid ideologies or axioms of rights and wrongs. According to Bollas,

> under certain circumstances, such axioms, which are based on ordinary psychological features that exist within us all, may evolve into patterns on customs of thought, eventually becoming organizing structures that will automatically generate mentalities or forms of behavior within a society. (p. xx)

Bollas builds on scholars and analysts who attended to pivotal social turning points in history. For example, summarizing the work of the French scholar Le Bon, Bollas noted that Le Bon's work on the psychology of the crowds emphasized that groups of individuals can become gripped by the social unconscious processes (i.e., demand for wars or violence toward certain groups) that deny or contradict personal values (i.e., human compassion, connection to others). Bollas noted that these writers highlighted the manic aspects of such unconscious processes, leading to groups' energizing proselytizing fervor and corresponding sense of unreality and depression.

Fractured states inside, splitting ourselves into "good" and "bad" or "positive" and "negative" which further resulted in not only fractured sense of self but also the society, which continually required the repression, dissociation, and denial of any undesirable trait in oneself or one's group while projecting these into people perceived as different. To achieve these goals, Bollas proposed the term of the "normopathic self" which continually seeks positivity and denials of personal or collective differences (p. 43). This idealized normopathic self, Bollas asserted, can never sustain its idealized processes, thus paradoxically resulting in a "compound" and "fractured" self where unacceptable states are perceived as uncontrollable obsessions or addictions (p. 46). In today's world, Bollas suggested, we also manufacture "transmissive" selves, selves that create a certain vision of selves and the world in order to transmit it to others, usually through media and social media (p. 51).

Bollas' assertions in relation to global world and immigration reflect potently cogent psychoanalytic arguments, noting that "there have been many different ways of living alongside one another in what we still call a society" (p. 73). He argued that instead of a vision of inclusivity, relationality, and multiplicity (which characterizes a healthy internal self-state and healthy communal states), individuals as well as societies have been "co-opted in support of a xenophobic retreat into regional, ethnic, religious or political enclaves... a self's retreat from the non-familiar world into the enclave of the secluded self" (p. 78). Bollas' assertion is that a democratic inclusive society requires the presence of individuals who are willing to accept their own internal democracy or presence of different, seemingly unacceptable states, rather than retreating into paranoias, rigid ideologies, and manias of optimism. In Bollas' view, "the examined life... looking into selves and their societies in order to gain insight into those mental and social forces that paralyse us" require an intentional "use of psychological understanding." This consideration is grounded in the capacity to withstand the common cultural "psychophobia" (i.e. fear of knowing our internal world), work toward the "creation of meaning" as well as the expression of "regret" in order to find "a new form of collective understanding in which humans can turn once again toward becoming humane beings" (pp. 127–128).

Confronting Xenophobia Through Post-colonial, De-colonial and Other Critical Theories

Many of the theories also emphasize possibilities for addressing or challenging xenophobia. Bhabha's (1984/2012, 1996) notion of ambivalence which often characterizes relationship between colonizer and the colonized, those in position to discriminate and those who are discriminated against, highlighted possibilities that those in power often vacillate between their desire to exploit and desire to be charitable. This uncertain or hybrid position, according to Bhabha (1995), can create disturbance in the otherwise established relations of domination and being dominated, making visible "the borderline, the marginal, the unclassifiable, the doubtful" (p. 161). According to Bhabha (1994),

> It is significant that the productive capacities of this Third Space have a colonial or postcolonial provenance. For a willingness to descend into that alien territory... may open the way to conceptualizing an *inter*national [sic] culture, based notion the exoticism of multiculturalism or the *diversity* of cultures, but on the inscription and articulation of cultures' *hybridity*. (p. 38)

In order to challenge xenophobia, it may be important, using Bhabha's (1994, 1996) theories, to de-historicize (i.e., challenge dominant histories) and de-locate (i.e., challenge notions of distinct borders, racial, national, and genetic differences) cultures.

Another de-colonial scholar Said (1983) proposed the move from filiation (emphasis on supposedly shared heredity) to affiliation (capacity to recognize complex interrelated connections with others). Like Bhabha, Said (1993) insisted on the importance of challenging dominant histories through what he called "contrapuntal readings" (i.e., examining all the scholarly, cultural, and political discourse for communication of prejudice and imperial domination) (p. 60).

Bhabha, Said and other postcolonial scholars insisted on a concept of liminality that permits to create what are called "borderlands" or spaces where binary views are challenged (Anzaldúa, 1987). Using these concepts, Pratt (1991) proposed the concept of the contact zone, which invites individuals to focus on differences, subjectivity, capacity to question, and ability to acknowledge clashes. Whereas these scholars have insisted that immigrants have created borderline and liminal spaces by their introduction of diverse opinions, cultural practices, and worldviews, creating intentional contact zones may also be important for individuals with dominant views. Ahmed (2013) similarly highlighted that an embodied, one-to-one subjective experience of "strangers" can offer an encounter that can become transformative as well as personally and collectively transgressive.

References

A Convocation of Bigots: The 1998 American Renaissance Conference. (1998). *The Journal of Blacks in Higher Education, 21*, 120–124.

Adorno, T. W., Frenkel-Brunswik, E., Levinson, D. J., & Sanford, R. N. (1950). *The authoritarian personality*. New York: Harper & Row.

Ahmed, S. (2013). *Strange encounters: Embodied others in post-coloniality*. London, UK: Routledge.

Akhtar, S. (2010). *Immigration and acculturation: Mourning, adaptation, and the next generation*. Lanham, UK: Jason Aronson.

Allport, G. W. (1954). *The nature of prejudice*. Reading, MA: Addison-Wesley.
Altemeyer, B. (1981). *Right-wing authoritarianism*. Winnipeg, ON, Canada: University of Manitoba Press.
Altemeyer, B. (1988). *Enemies of freedom: Understanding right-wing authoritarianism*. San Francisco, CA: Jossey-Bass.
Anzaldúa, G. (1987). *Borderlands: La frontera* (Vol. 3). San Francisco, CA: Aunt Lute.
Bales, K., & Soodalter, R. (2010). *The slave next door: Human trafficking and slavery in America today*. Berkeley, CA: University of California Press.
Baldwin, J. (1965). White man's guilt. *Ebony Magazine*, 47–48.
Baldwin, J. (1998). *Collected essays*. New York: Library of America.
Bashford, A., & Levine, P. (Eds.). (2010). *The Oxford handbook of the history of eugenics*. New York: Oxford University Press.
Bhabha, H. (1990). *DissemiNation: Time, narrative, and the margins of the modern nation*. London: Routledge.
Bhabha, H. K. (1994). *The location of culture*. London: Routledge.
Bhabha, H. K. (1995). *Nation and narration*. London: Routledge.
Bhabha, H. K. (1996). Culture's in-between. *Questions of Cultural Identity, 1*, 53–60.
Bhabha, H. K. (1984/2012). *The location of culture*. New York, NY: Routledge.
Bollas, C. (2018). *Meaning and melancholia: Life in the age of bewilderment*. Abingdon, UK: Routledge.
Bosma, U. (2007). Beyond the Atlantic: Connecting migration and world history in the age of imperialism, 1840–1940. *International Review of Social History, 52*(1), 116–123.
Bouchard, T. J. (1996). Galton lecture: Behaviour genetic studies of intelligence, yesterday and today: The long journey from plausibility to proof. *Journal of Biosocial Science, 28*(4), 527–555.
Bouie, J. (2013). Immigrants' IQ lower, wrote co-author of Heritage Foundation report. *The Daily Beast*. Retrieved from https://www.thedailybeast.com/immigrants-iq-lower-wrote-coathor-of-heritage-foundation-report?ref=scroll.
Brigham, C. C. (1923). *A study of American intelligence*. Princeton, NJ: Princeton University Press.
Buck, B., Hobbs, M., Kaiser, A., Lang, S., Montero, D., Romines, K., et al. (2003). Immigration and immigrants: Trends in American public opinion, 1964–1999. *Journal of Ethnic & Cultural Diversity in Social Work, 12*, 73–90.
Buss, D. M. (1994). *The evolution of desire: Strategies for human mating*. New York: Basic Books.
Buss, D. M. (2009). The great struggles of life: Darwin and the emergence of evolutionary psychology. *American Psychologist, 64*(2), 140.
Buss, D. M. (2016). *The evolution of desire: Strategies of human mating*. New York, NY: Basic books.

Cacho, L. M. (2000). 'The people of California are suffering': The ideology of white injury in discourses of immigration. *Journal for Cultural Research, 4*(4), 389–418.
Casey, E. S., & Watkins, M. (2014). *Up against the wall: Re-imagining the US-Mexico border.* Austin, TX: University of Texas Press.
Cogdell, C. (2010). *Eugenic design: Streamlining America in the 1930s.* Philadelphia, PA: University of Pennsylvania Press.
Currell, S., & Cogdell, C. (Eds.). (2006). *Popular eugenics: National efficiency and American mass culture in the 1930s.* Athens, OH: Ohio University Press.
Dalal, F. (2002). *Race, colour and the processes of racialization: New perspectives from psychoanalysis, group analysis and sociology.* Hove and New York: Brunner-Routledge.
Darwin, C. (1859). *On the origin of species: Or, the preservation of favoured races in the struggle for life.* London: Down, Bromley, Kent.
Darwin, C. (1898). *The life and letters of Charles Darwin, including an autobiographical chapter* (Rev. ed., F. Darwin, Ed.). London, UK: John Murray.
Davis, J. H. (2018, June 15). Separated at the border from their parents: In six weeks, 1,995 children. *New York Times.* Retrieved from https://www.nytimes.com/2018/06/15/us/politics/trump-immigration-separation-border.html.
Dawkins, R. (1981). Selfish genes in race or politics. *Nature, 289,* 528.
Deloria, V. (1997). *Red earth, white lies: Native Americans and the myth of scientific fact.* Golden, CO: Fulcrum Publishing.
Du Bois, W. E. B. (1903). *The talented tenth.* New York, NY: James Pott and Company.
Ensor, J. (2016). "Photo of my son has changed nothing," Says father of drowned Syrian refugee boy Alan Kurdi. *The Telegraph.* Retrieved from https://www.telegraph.co.uk/news/2016/09/01/photo-of-my-dead-son-has-changed-nothing-says-father-of-drowned.
Ervin, N. (1994). Immigration and the environment. In N. Mills (Ed.), *Arguing immigration: Are new immigrants a wealth of diversity… or a crushing burden?* (pp. 90–96). New York: Simon & Schuster.
Falkner, J., Schaller, M., Park, J. H., & Duncan, L. A. (2004). Evolved disease-avoidance mechanisms and contemporary xenophobic attitudes. *Group Processes & Intergroup Relations, 7,* 333–353.
Fanon, F. (1959/2008). *Black skin/White masks.* New York: Grove Press.
Fausto-Sterling, A. (1993). The five sexes. *The Sciences, 33*(2), 20–24.
Freud, S. (1909). Analysis of a phobia in a five-year-old boy. In *The standard edition of the complete psychological works of Sigmund Freud, volume X (1909): Two case histories ('Little Hans' and the 'Rat Man')* (pp. 1–150). London: Hogarth Press.
Freud, S. (1930). *Civilization and its discontents* (Standard Edition). London: Hogarth Press.

Freud, S. (1953). *The standard edition of the complete psychological works of Sigmund Freud* (Trans. From the German by J. Strachey, A. Freud, & A. Richards). London: Hogarth Press.

Freud, S. (1964). *Complete psychological works of Sigmund Freud.* Standard edition. (Trans. by K. Strachey). London: Hogarth Press.

Frosh, S. (2004). Freud, psychoanalysis and anti-semitism. *Psychoanalytic Review, 91*(3), 309–330. https://doi.org/10.1521/prev.91.3.309.38302.

Fry, B. N. (2001). *Responding to immigration: Perceptions of promise and threat.* New York: LFB Scholarly Publishers.

Furnham, A. (1992). Relationship between knowledge of and attitudes towards AIDS. *Psychological Reports, 71*(3), 1149–1150.

Galton, F. (1865). Hereditary talent and character. *Macmillan's Magazine, 12*(157), 318–327.

Galton, F. (1869). *Hereditary genius: An inquiry into its laws and consequences.* New York: Macmillan.

Galton, F. (1883). *Inquiries into the human faculty & its development.* London: J.M. Dent.

Goddard, H. H. (1911). The elimination of feeble-mindedness. *The Annals of the American Academy of Political and Social Science, 37*(2), 261–272.

Goddard, H. H. (1919). *Psychology of the normal and subnormal.* New York: Dodd, Mead.

Gomez, A. (2016). *Another election surprise: Many Hispanics back Trump.* Retrieved from https://www.usatoday.com/story/news/politics/elections/2016/2016/11/09/hispanic-vote-election-2016-donald-trump-hillary-clinton/93540772/.

Gottfredson, L. S. (2005). Suppressing intelligence research: Hurting those we intend to help. In R. H. Wright & N. A. Cummings (Eds.), *Destructive trends in mental health: The well-intentioned path to harm* (pp. 155–186). New York, NY: Routledge.

Gottfredson, L. S. (2012). Resolute ignorance on race and Rushton. *Personality and Individual Differences, 55,* 218–223. https://doi.org/10.1016/j.paid.2012.10.021.

Gould, S. J. (1995). *The mismeasure of man.* New York, NY: W.W. Norton & Company.

Gozdziak, E. M., & Collett, E. A. (2005). Research on human trafficking in North America: A review of literature. *International Migration, 43*(1–2), 99–128.

Gur-Arie, R. (2014). American Eugenics Society (1926–1972). *Embryo Project Encyclopedia.* http://embryo.asu.edu/handle/10776/8241.

Hall, G. S. (1903). The white man's burden versus indigenous development of the lower races. *The Journal of Education, 58*(4, 1438), 83.

Hall, G. S. (1909). Evolution and psychology. In E. B. Poulton & G. S. Hall (Eds.), *Fifty years of Darwinism: Modern aspects of evolution* (pp. 251–267). Boston: H. Holt.

Hatewatch. (2013). *Co-author of new immigration study says Latinos not as intelligent.* Retrieved from https://www.splcenter.org/hatewatch/2013/05/08/co-author-new-immigration-study-says-latinos-not-intelligent.

Helms, J. E. (Ed.). (1990). *Black and White racial identity: Theory, research and practice.* Westport, CT: Greenwood.

Ioanide, P. (2014). The alchemy of race and affect: "White innocence" and public secrets in the post-civil rights era. *Kalfou, 1*(1), 151–168.

Jost, J. T., & Banaji, M. R. (1994). The role of stereotyping in system-justification and he production of false consciousness. *British Journal of Social Psychology, 33,* 1–27.

Jost, J. T., Banaji, M. R., & Nosek, B. A. (2004). A decade of system justification theory: Accumulated evidence of conscious and unconscious bolstering of the status quo. *Political Psychology, 25*(6), 881–919.

Kanazawa, S., & Frerichs, R. L. (2001). Why single men might abhor foreign cultures. *Social Biology, 48,* 321–328.

Kuhl, S. (2002). *The Nazi connection: Eugenics, American racism, and German national socialism.* New York: Oxford University Press.

Lacan, J. (1978/1998). *The four fundamental concepts of psycho-analysis.* New York, NY: W.W. Norton & Company.

Layton, L. (2009). Who's responsible? Our mutual implication in each other's suffering. *Psychoanalytic Dialogues, 19*(2), 105–120.

Layton, L. (2010). Irrational exuberance: Neoliberal subjectivity and the perversion of truth. *Subjectivity, 3*(3), 303–322.

Le Espiritu, Y. (2003). *Home bound: Filipino American lives across cultures, communities, and countries.* Berkeley, CA: University of California Press.

LeMay, M. C. (2004). *U.S. immigration: A reference handbook.* Santa Barbara, CA: ABC CLIO.

Lerner, M. (1980). *The belief in a just world: A fundamental delusion.* New York, NY: Plenum Press.

Levinas, E. (1996). *Emmanuel Levinas: Basic philosophical writings.* Bloomington, IN: Indiana University Press.

Lipsitz, G. (2006). *The possessive investment in whiteness: How white people profit from identity politics.* Philadelphia, PA: Temple University Press.

Lombardo, P. A. (Ed.). (2011). *A century of eugenics in America: From the Indiana experiment to the human genome era.* Bloomington, IN: Indiana University Press.

Lynn, R. (2001). *Eugenics: A reassessment.* New York: Praeger.

Lyons, P. D., & Clark, J. J. (2008). Interaction, enculturation, social distance, and ancient ethnic identities. In L. D. Webster, M. E. McBrinn, & E. Gamboa Carrera (Eds.), *Archaeology without borders: Contact, commerce, and change in the US Southwest and Northwestern Mexico* (pp. 185–207). Boulder: University Press of Colorado.

MacDonald, K. (2005). Personality, evolution, and development. Evolutionary perspectives on human development. In R. L. Burgess, R. G. Burgess, & K. MacDonald (Eds.), *Evolutionary perspectives on human development* (pp. 207–242). Thousand Oaks, CA: Sage.

McKinnon, S. (2005). *Neo-liberal genetics: The myths and moral tales of evolutionary psychology*. Chicago, IL: Prickly Paradigm Press.

McKinnon, S., & Silverman, S. (Eds.). (2005). *Complexities: Beyond nature and nurture*. Chicago, IL: University of Chicago Press.

Merskin, D. L. (2011). *Media, minorities, and meaning: A critical introduction*. New York: Peter Lang.

Mills, N. (Ed.). (1994). *Arguing immigration: Are new immigrants a wealth of diversity... or a crushing burden?* New York: Simon & Schuster.

National Genome Research Association. (2006). *Whole genome association studies*. Retrieved from https://www.genome.gov/17516714/2006-release-about-whole-genome-association-studies/.

Ommundsen, R., & Larsen, K. S. (1997). Attitudes toward illegal aliens: The reliability and validity of a Likert-type scale. *Journal of Social Psychology, 137*, 665–667.

Ommundsen, R., Van der Veer, K., Yakushko, O., & Ullenberg, P. (2013). Exploring the relationships between fear-based xenophobia, social contact, and perceptions of out-group entitativity in Norway. *Psychological Reports, 112*(1), 109–124.

Ott, E. M. (1995). Effects of the male female ration at work: Policewomen and male nurses. *Psychology of Women Quarterly, 13*, 41–57.

Patterson, O. (1982). *Slavery and social death*. Cambridge, MA: Harvard University Press.

Pearson, K. (1905). *National life from the standpoint of science*. London: Adam and Black.

Pearson, K. (1911). *The scope and importance to the state of the science of national eugenics*. London: Dulau and Company.

Perea, J. F. (1997). Introduction. In J. F. Perea (Ed.), *Immigrants out! The new nativism and the anti-immigrant impulse in the United States* (pp. 1–12). New York: New York University Press.

Pew Hispanic Center. (2016). *Occupations of unauthorized immigrants*. Retrieved from http://www.pewhispanic.org/2016/11/03/occupations-of-unauthorized-immigrant-workers/.

Pinker, S. (2002). *The blank slate: The modern denial of human nature*. New York, NY: Penguin.

Pinker, S. (2005). Sex ed. *The New Republic*. Retrieved May 18, 2018, from https://newrepublic.com/article/68044/sex-ed.

Pinker, S. (2018). *Enlightenment now: The case for reason, science, humanism, and progress*. New York: Penguin.

Pioneer Fund. (2013). Website archived at https://web.archive.org/web/20130412144849/http://www.pioneerfund.org/.

Pratt, M. L. (1991). Arts of the contact zone. *Profession, 91*, 33–40.

Pratto, F., Sidanius, J., Stallworth, L. M., & Malle, B. F. (1994). Social dominance orientation: A personality variable predicting social and political attitudes. *Journal of Personality and Social Psychology, 67*, 741–763.

Reynolds, V., & Vine, I. (1987). *The socio-biology of ethnocentrism: Evolutionary dimensions of xenophobia, discrimination, racism, and nationalism*. London: Croom Helm.

Runciman, W. G. (1966). *Relative deprivation and social justice: A study of attitudes to social inequality in twentieth-century England*. Berkeley: University of California Press.

Rushton, P. (2000). Speech at the American renaissance conference. Quote retrieved from Southern Poverty Law Center website at https://www.splcenter.org/fighting-hate/extremist-files/individual/jean-philipperushton.

Rushton, J. P. (1990). Sir Francis Galton, epigenetic rules, genetic similarity theory, and human life-history analysis. *Journal of Personality, 58*(1), 117–140.

Rushton, J. P. (1995). *Race, evolution, and behavior*. New Brunswick, NJ: Transaction.

Rushton, J. P. (1999). Genetic similarity theory and the nature of ethnocentrism. In K. Thienpont & R. Cliquet (Eds.), *In-group/out-group behavior in modern societies: An evolutionary perspective*. Amsterdam, The Netherlands: Vlaamse Gemeeschap/CBGS.

Rushton, J. P. (2005). Ethnic nationalism, evolutionary psychology and genetic similarity theory. *Nations and Nationalism, 11*(4), 489–507.

Rushton, J. P., & Jensen, A. R. (2005). Wanted: More race realism, less moralistic fallacy. *Psychology, Public Policy, and Law, 11*(2), 328–336. https://doi.org/10.1037/1076-8971.11.2.328.

Ruti, M. (2015). *The age of scientific sexism: How evolutionary psychology promotes gender profiling and fans the battle of the sexes*. Toronto, ON, Canada: Bloomsbury Publishing.

Rydgren, J. (2004). The logic of xenophobia. *Rationality and Society, 16*, 123–148.

Said, E. W. (1983). *The world, the text, and the critic*. Cambridge, MA: Harvard University Press.

Said, E. (1993). The politics of knowledge. In C. McCarthy & W. Crichlow (Eds.), *Race, identify and representation in education* (pp. 306–314). New York: Routledge.

Sartre, J. P. (1943/1956). *Being and Nothingness* (Trans. by Hazel E. Barnes). New York, NY: Philosophical Library.

Seely, M. (2012). *Born expecting the pleistocene: Psychology and the problem of civilization*. Cobham, UK: Old Dog books.

Selden, S. (1999). *Inheriting shame: The story of eugenics and racism in America*. New York: Teachers College Press.

Shelley, L. (2010). *Human trafficking: A global perspective*. Cambridge, UK: Cambridge University Press.

Sherif, M., Harvey, O. J., White, B. J., Hood, W. R., & Sherif, C. W. (1961). *Intergroup cooperation and conflict: The robbers cave experiment*. Norman, OK: University of Oklahoma Book Exchange.

Silva, E. B. (2003). *Racism without racists: Color-blind racism and the persistence of racial inequality in the United States*. Lanham, MD: Rowman & Littlefield.

Social Biology. (1973). A new name society for the study of social biology (Formerly the American Eugenics Society). *Social Biology, 20*(1), 1. https://doi.org/10.1080/19485565.1973.9988017.

Southern Poverty Law Center. (2017). *The Pioneer Fund*. Retrieved November 2, 2018, from https://www.splcenter.org/fighting-hate/extremist-files/group/pioneer-fund.

Southern Poverty Law Center. (2018). *Jean-Philippe Rushton*. Retrieved November 2, 2018, from https://www.splcenter.org/fighting-hate/extremist-files/individual/jean-philippe-rushton.

Spivak, G. (2013). *The Spivak reader: Selected works of Gayati Chakravorty Spivak*. London, UK: Routledge.

Steele, S. (1990). White guilt. *American Scholar, 59*, 497–506.

Stephan, W. G., & Stephan, C. W. (1996). *Intergroup relations*. Boulder, CO: Westview Press.

Stephan, C. W., & Stephan, W. S. (2013). An integrated threat theory of prejudice. In S. Oskamp (Ed.). *Reducing prejudice and discrimination* (pp. 33–56). New York: Psychology Press.

Stephan, W. G., Ybarra, O., & Bachman, G. (1999). Prejudice toward immigrants: An integrated threat theory. *Journal of Applied Social Psychology, 29*, 2221–2237.

Tactaquin, C. (1998). The greening of the anti-immigrant agenda. *Network News*, Spring Issue.

Tatum, B. D. (1994). Teaching White students about racism: The search for White allies and the restoration of hope. *Teacher College Record, 95*, 462–476.

Thornton, M. C., & Mizuno, Y. (1999). Economic well-being and Black adult feelings toward immigrants and Whites, 1984. *Journal of Black Studies, 30*, 15–44.

Tucker, W. H. (1996). *The science and politics of racial research*. Urbana-Champaign: University of Illinois Press.

U.S. Citizen and Immigration Services. (2018). *Green Card eligibility categories*. https://www.uscis.gov/greencard/eligibility-categories.

U.S. Congress. (2004). *Mail-order bride business*. U.S. Legal Code, Title 8, Chapter 12, Subchapter II, Part IX, § 1375. Retrieved August 16, 2006, from http://www4.law.cornell.edu/uscode/html/uscode08/usc_sec08_00001375-000-.html.

van den Berghe, P. L. (1999). Racism, ethnocentrism, and xenophobia: In our genes or in our memes? In K. Thienpont & R. Cliquet (Eds.), *In-group/out-group behavior in modern societies*. Amsterdam, The Netherlands: NIDI CBGS Publications.

van der Dennen, J. M. G. (1987). Ethnocentrism and in-group/out-group differentiation: A review and interpretation of the literature. In V. Reynolds, V. S. E. Falger, & I. Vine (Eds.), *The sociobiology of ethnocentrism: Evolutionary dimensions of xenophobia, discrimination, racism, and nationalism* (pp. 1–47). London: Croom Helm.

Van der Veer, K., Ommundsen, R., Yakushko, O., & Higler, L. (2011). Cross-national measure of fear-based xenophobia: Development of a cumulative scale. *Psychological Reports, 109*(1), 27–42. https://doi.org/10.2466/07.17.pro.109.4.

Van der Veer, K., Ommundsen, R., Yakushko, O., Higler, L., Woelders, S., & Hagen, K. A. (2013). Psychometrically and qualitatively validating a cross-national cumulative measure of fear-based xenophobia. *Quality and Quantity in Psychology, 47,* 1423–1444.

Wilson, E. O. (1975). *Sociobiology: The new synthesis*. Cambridge, MA: Harvard University Press.

Williamson, J. (1997). Globalization and inequality, past and present. *The World Bank Research Observer, 12,* 117–135.

Wistrich, R. S. (2011). *Demonizing the other: Antisemitism, racism, and xenophobia*. London, UK: Routledge.

Yakushko, O. (2009a). Human trafficking: A review for mental health professionals. *International Journal for the Advancement of Counselling, 31,* 158–167. https://doi.org/10.1007/s10447-009-9075-3.

Yakushko, O. (2009b). Xenophobia: Understanding the roots and consequences of negative attitudes towards immigrants. *The Counseling Psychologist, 37,* 36–66.

Yakushko, O., & Rajan, I. (2017). Global love for sale: Divergence and convergence of human trafficking with "Mail Order Brides" and international arranged marriage phenomena. *Women & Therapy, 40*(1–2), 190–206.

Yerkes, R. M. (1923). Eugenic bearing of measurements of intelligence. *The Eugenics Review, 14*(4), 225–229.

Zylinska, J. (2004). The universal acts: Judith Butler and the biopolitics of immigration. *Cultural Studies, 18*(4), 523–537.

CHAPTER 5

How to Welcome a Stranger

Abstract Based on history and theories in regard to xenophobia and anti-immigrant prejudice, this chapter presents suggestions for how to challenge this form of social oppression. Specifically, this chapter discusses ways of humanizing immigrants, attending to history of social oppression, and creating opportunities for genuine social connections between native- and foreign-born communities, which may countract xenophobic prejudice and violence.

Keywords Social change · Social justice · Immigrant integration

Xenophobia is among the most pernicious forms of contemporary prejudice toward others who are perceived as different. While not historical or universal among human communities, it has characterized relation to immigrants and foreigners in many cultures. One of the more malicious aspects of justifying xenophobia is biologizing and universalizing this form of prejudice, such as in those who employ social Darwinism, eugenics, and contemporary "evolutionary" theories of differences. Similarly to justifying racism and sexism by social Darwinist, eugenicists, and other scientists of human difference, these "theoretical" contributions rationalize and substantiate this form of prejudice. Similar to the 1951 *UNESCO Statement of the Nature of Race and Racial Difference*,

O. Yakushko, *Modern-Day Xenophobia*,
https://doi.org/10.1007/978-3-030-00644-0_5

while biological differences can always be noted among many groups (i.e., races, genders, ethnicities), providing so-called scientific rationalizations for what are essentially environmental, cultural, social, and historical distinctions are unacceptable.

In addition, like other forms of prejudice, xenophobia is proposed to reflect apparently realistic or accurate human attitudes while, in fact, reproducing false stereotypical and fictitious views of individual groups. These views contribute to, reinforce, and underlie immigrants' social death. Moreover, xenophobia, similar to all forms of prejudice, require splitting them into all-good (i.e., hard-working, happy or nerds) or all-bad (i.e., "wretched refuse," criminal, immoral) people. This splitting, reflecting psychologically crude defenses, requires that immigrants remain either child-like, needing help, and desperate (i.e., "wretched refuse") to maintain a relationship that perceives them as dependent, unthreatening, and deprived. This immigrant position requires the native-born individual either to respond with supposed empathy and help or (more likely) evoke unconscious or implicit resentment of giving out previous personal and collective resources away from native-born people. To illustrate, the reader could consider the response to a neighbor that experiences a life-threatening event versus an immigrant, perceived as experiencing a life-threatening event. Reader's potential responses to a neighbour are unlikely to include severe judgments (e.g., what did you do to deserve this?), are unlikely to be condescending and patronizing (e.g., what a wretch you are needing our help!), and are unlikely to consciously feel resentful that this neighbor's plight as somehow damaging one's own personal resources (e.g., you are using up resources that should go to me or my family). In addition, elevating one's neighbor to be the absolute best in any category (e.g., a model neighbor like a model immigrant) is likely to feel unrealistic and forced. Both theorists such as Ahmed (2013) and empirical scholars such as Ommundsen, Van der Veer, Yakushko, and Ullenberg (2013) emphasized that any shifts in relationship to immigrants and immigrant community cannot occur through merely more contact but through interactions that equalize and relate foreigners and the native-born in meaningful sustained ways.

In fact, most of us do not perceive other human beings as either personal charity cases or as paragons of all virtue—such judgments would reflect severe pathologies on our part as well as result in problematic social relations (Ahmed, 2013; Bollas, 2018; Freud, 1930; Layton, 2010). Yet, it is precisely the splitting and projections native-born individuals engage in in relation to immigrants who are dehumanized in these ways, claiming them either a threat or an inferior depended altruism proof. In fact, the eugenicist and founder of American psychology Stanley G. Hall in his 1921 *Jesus the Christ in Light of Psychology* condescendingly proclaimed that the eugenically unfit might have a very special evolutionary reason for existence: teaching the eugenically fit individuals how to be moral and charitable by being around the poor and wretched evolutionary unfit people. People claimed to be the lesser human beings—the aliens, the "animals," the unfit, the strangers—are not full human beings worthy of full human rights, agency, rights, and opportunities. Instead, they serve as conduits for the dominant or (in case of xenophobia, native-born) people's individual (authentic) happiness by dispensing their generosity and maintaining their own conscious façade of being moral, altruistic. In words of an evolutionary psychologist Steven Pinker (2011), who routinely supports oppression as an invariable evolutonary necessity, such moral condescention toward those considered less privileged by the evolution supposedly leads people to become "the better angels of our nature" (title).

Thus, based on critical theories of prejudice, I propose several strategies for addressing xenophobia. First, immigrants must be made human. Humanizing immigrants requires that they are perceived as genuine human beings whose behavior and experiences reflect the complexity of what it means to be human: having sorrow about being traumatized, having anger about being marginalized, rather than being silenced, normalized, made transmissive or fetishized, or criminalized. Immigrants like all human beings are products of historical and contemporary social worlds, including the liberatory and oppressive, cooperative and aggressive, progressive and regressive. Their experiences will reflect profoundly complex relations of worldviews, expectations of home and host cultures, as well as many fantasies about who they are and what they are meant to do.

Another move in addressing xenophobia is to historicize and contextualize immigration. Reasons for immigration, reactions to immigrants, and context of globalization are vital to consider in order to humanize immigrants and to challenge xenophobia. Past and present international conflicts, neoliberal capitalist world politics and economic patterns, and interactive influences of environmental and social crises on migration all have a role in the movement of people across national borders. This complexity is fascinating, interesting, and dynamic—reading this history is likely to evoke a sense of guilt and shame as well as awe, respect, and interconnectedness with people around the globe. Thus, another important step is to harness the horror and humility by recognizing the horror of both conditions that make individuals move across borders, especially without legal protection, or humility or genuine sense of guilt in relation to how dominant cultures often create immigration and then punish the immigrants.

The final suggestion is to permit immigrant subjectivity by inviting immigrant stories while knowing that their stories may reflect the dominant discourse, that they must be always happy, compliant, hardworking and silent. Working toward the genuine stories will be more challenging and arduous but offering much greater possibilities of humanizing immigrants and migration. Immigrants are already creating spaces for such stories through the liminal borderline constructions: their art, music, literature, foods, religion, and more. Liberation perspectives permit immigrants themselves to define what it means to be an immigrant, and how such self-constructions are always hybrid, nonlinear, and socially constructed.

Addressing xenophobia may offer another opportunity to challenge the cultural norms of demonizing, splitting, defining as unfit, and otherizing of not just immigrants but all other groups. As I noted in the introductory remarks, immigrants already represent this diversity—they are racially, gender, sexuality, ethnically, religiously, social class, age and otherwise different according to other multiple human categories. Like most of these other categories, they are illusionary, historically constructed and socially meaningful while neither valid nor accurate.

In nature and many human societies, possibilities of human collaboration and interconnection, possibilities of engaging with difference toward richness and multiplicity, and development through diversity. Challenging xenophobia is also a pathway toward challenging our own psychophobias or the fear of our own inner complexity, diversity, and humane humanity. More importantly, challenging xenophobia can counteract or (hopefully) diminish profound physical, psychological, political, and social violence directed toward all the human beings who migrate across the borders.

References

Ahmed, S. (2013). *Strange encounters: Embodied others in post-coloniality.* London, UK: Routledge.

Bollas, C. (2018). *Meaning and melancholia: Life in the age of bewilderment.* Abingdon, UK: Routledge.

Freud, S. (1930). *Civilization and its discontents* (Standard Edition). London: Hogarth Press.

Layton, L. (2010). Irrational exuberance: Neoliberal subjectivity and the perversion of truth. *Subjectivity, 3*(3), 303–322.

Ommundsen, R., Van der Veer, K., Yakushko, O., & Ullenberg, Pal. (2013). Exploring the relationships between fear-based xenophobia, social contact, and perceptions of out-group entitativity in Norway. *Psychological Reports, 112*(1), 109–124.

Pinker, S. (2011). *The better angels of our nature: The decline of violence in history and its causes.* London, UK: Penguin.

References

A Convocation of Bigots: The 1998 American Renaissance Conference. (1998). *The Journal of Blacks in Higher Education, 21*, 120–124.

Abromeit, J., Norman, Y., Marotta, G., & Chesterton, B. M. (Eds.). (2015). *Transformations of populism in Europe and the Americas: History and recent tendencies*. London, UK: Bloomsbury.

Addison, T., & Worswick, C. (2002). The impact of immigration on the earnings of natives: Evidence from Australian micro data. *Economic Record, 78*(240), 68–78.

Adorno, T. W., Frenkel-Brunswik, E., Levinson, D. J., & Sanford, R. N. (1950). *The authoritarian personality*. New York: Harper & Row.

Ahmed, S. (2013). *Strange encounters: Embodied others in post-coloniality*. London, UK: Routledge.

Akhtar, S. (2010). *Immigration and acculturation: Mourning, adaptation, and the next generation*. Lanham, UK: Jason Aronson.

Akresh, I. R. (2008). Occupational trajectories of legal US immigrants: Downgrading and recovery. *Population and Development Review, 34*(3), 435–456.

Alexander, P. (1987). *Racism, resistance, and revolution*. London: Bookmarks.

Allport, G. W. (1954). *The nature of prejudice*. Reading, MA: Addison-Wesley.

Altemeyer, B. (1981). *Right-wing authoritarianism*. Winnipeg, ON, Canada: University of Manitoba Press.

Altemeyer, B. (1988). *Enemies of freedom: Understanding right-wing authoritarianism*. San Francisco: Jossey-Bass.

American Immigration Council. (2013). *The economic blame game: Immigration and unemployment*. Washington, DC: Immigration Policy Center. Retrieved June 2018, from https://www.americanimmigrationcouncil.org/sites/default/files/research/economic_blame_game.pdf.

O. Yakushko, *Modern-Day Xenophobia*,
https://doi.org/10.1007/978-3-030-00644-0

Ana, O. S. (1999). 'Like an animal I was treated': Anti-immigrant metaphor in US public discourse. *Discourse and Society, 10*(2), 191–224.

Anzaldúa, G. (1987). *Borderlands: La frontera* (Vol. 3). San Francisco: Aunt Lute.

Art, D. (2011). *Inside the radical right: The development of anti-immigrant parties in Western Europe*. Cambridge, UK: Cambridge University Press.

Aruga, T. (1994). Reflections on the history of US-Japanese relations. *American Studies International, 32*(1), 8–16.

Ashcroft, B. (2013). *Post-colonial transformation*. London: Routledge.

Austin-Hillery, N. (2018). Trump's racist language serves abusive immigration policies. *Human Rights Campaign Report*. Retrieved November 1, 2018, from https://www.hrw.org/news/2018/05/22/trumps-racistlanguage-serves-abusive-immigration-policies.

Baldwin, J. (1965). White man's guilt. *Ebony Magazine*, 47–48.

Baldwin, J. (1993). *Nobody knows my name: More notes of a native son*. New York, NY: Vintage.

Baldwin, J. (1998). *Collected essays*. New York: Library of America.

Bales, K., & Soodalter, R. (2010). *The slave next door: Human trafficking and slavery in America today*. Berkeley, CA: University of California Press.

Bashford, A., & Levine, P. (Eds.). (2010). *The Oxford handbook of the history of eugenics*. New York: Oxford University Press.

Bauder, H. (2003). "Brain abuse", or the devaluation of immigrant labour in Canada. *Antipode, 35*(4), 699–717.

Baumgartl, B., & Favell, A. (Eds.). (1995). *New xenophobia in Europe*. London: Kluwer Law International.

Bebout, L. (2016). *Whiteness on the border: Mapping the U.S. racial imagination in Brown and White*. New York, NY: New York University Press.

Berger, R. (2005). *Immigrant women tell their stories*. New York: The Haworth Press.

Bhabha, H. (1990). *DissemiNation: Time, narrative, and the margins of the modern nation*. London: Routledge.

Bhabha, H. K. (1983). The other question: Difference, discrimination and the discourses of colonialism. *Screen, 24*(6), 18–36. https://doi.org/10.1093/screen/24.6.18.

Bhabha, H. (1990). *DissemiNation: Time, narrative, and the margins of the modern nation*. London: Routledge.

Bhabha, H. K. (1994). *The location of culture*. London: Routledge.

Bhabha, H. K. (1995). *Nation and narration*. London: Routledge.

Bhabha, H. K. (1996). Culture's in-between. *Questions of Cultural Identity, 1*, 53–60.

Bhabha, H. K. (1984/2012). *The location of culture*. New York, NY: Routledge.

Black, E. (2003). *War against the weak: Eugenics and America's campaign to create a master race*. New York, NY: Four Walls Eight Windows Press.

Bobo, L. (1988). Group conflict, prejudice, and the paradox of contemporary racial attitudes. In P. A. Katz & D. A. Taylor (Eds.), *Eliminating racism: Profiles in controversy* (pp. 85–116). New York: Plenum.

Boehnke, K. (2001). *Report of the NGO working group on migration and xenophobia for the world conference on international migration, racism, discrimination and xenophobia.* A publication jointly produced by ILO, IOM, OHCHR, in consultation with UNHCR.

Boehnke, K., Hagan, J., & Hefler, G. (1998). On the development of xenophobia in Germany: The adolescent years. *Journal of Social Issues, 54,* 585–603.

Bolaffi, G. (Ed.). (2003). *Dictionary of race, ethnicity and culture.* Thousand Oaks, CA: Sage.

Bollas, C. (2018). *Meaning and melancholia: Life in the age of bewilderment.* Abingdon, UK: Routledge.

Bosma, U. (2007). Beyond the Atlantic: Connecting migration and world history in the age of imperialism, 1840–1940. *International Review of Social History, 52*(1), 116–123.

Bouchard, T. J. (1996). Galton lecture: Behaviour genetic studies of intelligence, yesterday and today: The long journey from plausibility to proof. *Journal of Biosocial Science, 28*(4), 527–555.

Bouie, J. (2013). Immigrants' IQ lower, wrote co-author of Heritage Foundation report. *The Daily Beast.* Retrieved from https://www.thedailybeast.com/immigrants-iq-lower-wrote-coathor-of-heritage-foundation-report?ref=scroll.

Bresnahan, M. J., Ohashi, R., Nebashi, R., Liu, W. Y., & Shearman, S. M. (2002). Attitudinal and affective response toward accented English. *Language and Communication, 22,* 171–185. https://doi.org/10.1016/S0271-5309(01)00025-8.

Brewer, M. B., & Campbell, D. T. (1976). *Ethnocentrism and intergroup attitudes.* New York: Wiley.

Brigham, C. C. (1923). *A study of American intelligence.* Princeton, NJ: Princeton University Press.

Buck, B., Hobbs, M., Kaiser, A., Lang, S., Montero, D., Romines, K., et al. (2003). Immigration and immigrants: Trends in American public opinion, 1964–1999. *Journal of Ethnic & Cultural Diversity in Social Work, 12,* 73–90.

Burke, P. (2005). *History and social theory.* Cambridge, UK: Polity.

Buss, D. M. (1994). *The evolution of desire: Strategies for human mating.* New York: Basic Books.

Buss, D. M. (2009). The great struggles of life: Darwin and the emergence of evolutionary psychology. *American Psychologist, 64*(2), 140.

Buss, D. M. (2016). *The evolution of desire: Strategies of human mating.* New York, NY: Basic books.

Cacho, L. M. (2000). 'The people of California are suffering': The ideology of white injury in discourses of immigration. *Journal for Cultural Research, 4*(4), 389–418.

Cacho, L. M. (2012). *Social death: Racialized rightlessness and the criminalization of the unprotected.* New York, NY: New York University Press.

Californians for Population Stabilization. (2018). https://www.capsweb.org/.

Carballo, D. M., Roscoe, P., & Feinman, G. M. (2014). Cooperation and collective action in the cultural evolution of complex societies. *Journal of Archaeological Method and Theory, 21*(1), 98–133.

Casey, E. S., & Watkins, M. (2014). *Up against the wall: Re-imagining the US-Mexico border.* Austin, TX: University of Texas Press.

Cashdan, E. (2001). Ethnocentrism and xenophobia: A cross-cultural study. *Current Anthropology, 42,* 760–765.

Castles, S., & Miller, M. J. (1993). *The age of migration: International population movements in the modern world.* London: Macmillan.

Chavez, L. R. (2001). *Covering immigration: Popular images and the politics of the nation.* Berkeley: University of California Press.

Chesterton, G. K. (1922). *Eugenics and other evils: An argument against the scientifically organized state.* London: Inkling Books.

Coenders, M., & Scheepers, P. (1998). Support for ethnic discrimination in the Netherlands. 1979–1993: Effects of period, cohort, and individual characteristics. *European Sociological Review, 14,* 404–422.

Cogdell, C. (2010). *Eugenic design: Streamlining America in the 1930s.* Philadelphia, PA: University of Pennsylvania Press.

Comas-Díaz, L., & Greene, B. (Eds.). (1994). *Women of color: Integrating ethnic and gender identities in psychotherapy.* New York: Guilford.

Comas-Diaz, L., & Greene, B. (1995). *Women of color.* New York: Guilford.

Connely, M. (2006, April 14). In polls, illegal immigrants are called burden. *New York Times,* p. A16.

Cowan, G., Martinez, L., & Mendiola, S. (1997). Predictors of attitudes toward illegal Latino immigrants. *Hispanic Journal of Behavioral Sciences, 19,* 403–415.

Creese, G., & Wiebe, B. (2012). 'Survival employment': Gender and deskilling among African immigrants in Canada. *International Migration, 50*(5), 56–76.

Crowther, J. (Ed.). (1995). *Oxford advanced learners dictionary of current English: International new students* (5th ed.). London: Oxford University Press.

Currell, S., & Cogdell, C. (Eds.). (2006). *Popular eugenics: National efficiency and American mass culture in the 1930s.* Athens, OH: Ohio University Press.

Curtin, P. (1984). *Cross-cultural trade in world history.* Cambridge: Cambridge University Press.

Dalal, F. (2002). *Race, colour and the processes of racialization: New perspectives from psychoanalysis, groupanalysis and sociology.* Hove and New York: Brunner-Routledge.

Dalal, F. (2009). The paradox of belonging. *Psychoanalysis, Culture & Society, 14*(1), 74–81.

Daley, J. (2016, November 29). Why xenophobia is Dictionary.com word of the year. *Smithsonian Smart News.* Retrieved from https://www.smithsonianmag.com/smart-news/why-xenophobia-dictionarycoms-word-year-180961225/.

Danieli, Y. (1984). Psychotherapist's participation in the conspiracy of silence about the Holocaust. *Psychoanalytic Psychology, 1*(1), 23.

Danieli, Y. (1985). The treatment and prevention of long-term effects and inter-generational transmission of victimization: A lesson from Holocaust survivors and their children. *Trauma and Its Wake, 1,* 295–313.

Daniels, R. (1977). *The politics of prejudice: The anti-Japanese movement in California and the struggle for Japanese exclusion.* Berkeley, CA: University of California Press.

Daniels, R. (2002). *Coming to America: A history of immigration and ethnicity in American life.* San Francisco: Harper Perennial.

Daniels, R. (2004). *Guarding the golden door: American immigration policy and immigrants since 1882.* New York: Hill and Wang.

Darwin, C. (1859). *On the origin of species: Or, the preservation of favoured races in the struggle for life.* London: Down, Bromley, Kent.

Darwin, C. (1888). *The descent of man and selection in relation to sex.* London: Murray.

Darwin, C. (1898). *The life and letters of Charles Darwin, including an autobiographical chapter* (Rev. ed., F. Darwin, Ed.). London, UK: John Murray.

Davenport, C. B. (1910). *Eugenics: The science of human improvement by better breeding.* New York: H. Holt.

Davis, J. H. (2018, June 15). Separated at the border from their parents: In six weeks, 1,995 children. *New York Times.* Retrieved from https://www.nytimes.com/2018/06/15/us/politics/trump-immigration-separation-border.html.

Dawkins, R. (1981). Selfish genes in race or politics. *Nature, 289,* 528.

Dean, J. A., & Wilson, K. (2009). 'Education? It is irrelevant to my job now. It makes me very depressed…': Exploring the health impacts of under/unemployment among highly skilled recent immigrants in Canada. *Ethnicity & Health, 14*(2), 185–204.

de Souza, L. E. C., Pereira, C. R., Camino, L., de Lima, T. J. S., & Torres, A. R. R. (2016). The legitimizing role of accent on discrimination against immigrants. *European Journal of Social Psychology, 46*(5), 609–620.

Deloria, V. (1997). *Red earth, white lies: Native Americans and the myth of scientific fact.* Golden, CO: Fulcrum Publishing.

Dodson, B. (2010). Locating xenophobia: Debate, discourse, and everyday experience in Cape Town, South Africa. *Africa Today, 56*(3), 2–22.

Du Bois, W. E. B. (1903). *The talented tenth.* New York, NY: James Pott and Company.

Duggan, L. (2012). *The twilight of equality?: Neoliberalism, cultural politics, and the attack on democracy.* Boston, MA: Beacon Press.

Dusek, V. (1999). Sociobiology sanitized: Evolutionary psychology and gene selectionism. *Science as Culture, 8*(2), 129–169.

Eckstein, Z., & Weiss, Y. (2004). On the wage growth of immigrants: Israel, 1990–2000. *Journal of the European Economic Association, 2*(4), 665–695.

Edwards, J. (1999). Refining our understanding of language attitudes. *Journal of Language and Social Psychology, 18*, 101–110. https://doi.org/10.1177/0261927X99018001007.

Elbagir, N., Razek, R., Platt, A., & Jones, B. (2016). People for sale. Exclusive report, *CNN*. Retrieved June 18, 2018, from https://edition.cnn.com/2017/11/14/africa/libya-migrant-auctions/index.html.

Ensor, J. (2016). "Photo of my son has changed nothing," Says father of drowned Syrian refugee boy Alan Kurdi. *The Telegraph*. Retrieved from https://www.telegraph.co.uk/news/2016/09/01/photo-of-my-dead-son-has-changed-nothing-says-father-of-drowned.

Ervin, N. (1994). Immigration and the environment. In N. Mills (Ed.), *Arguing immigration: Are new immigrants a wealth of diversity... or a crushing burden?* (pp. 90–96). New York: Simon & Schuster.

Espenshade, T. J. (2000). Immigrants, Puerto Ricans, and the earnings of native Black males. In G. D. Jaynes (Ed.), *Immigration and race: New challenges for American democracy* (pp. 125–142). New Haven, CT: Yale University Press.

Espanshade, T. J., & Calhoun, C. A. (1993). An analysis of public opinion toward undocumented migration. *Population Research and Policy Review, 12*, 189–224.

Esses, V. M., Dovidio, J. F., Jackson, L. M., & Armstrong, T. L. (2001). The immigration dilemma: The role of perceived group competition, ethnic prejudice, and national identity. *Journal of Social Issues, 57*, 389–412.

Esses, V. M., Dovidio, J. F., Semenya, A. H., & Jackson, L. M. (2005). Attitudes toward immigrants and immigration: The role of national and international identity. In D. Abrams, M. A. Hogg, & J. M. Marques, (Eds.), *The social psychology of inclusion and exclusion* (pp. 317–337). New York, NY: Psychology Press.

Esses, V. M., Haddock, G., & Zanna, M. P. (1993). Values, stereotypes, and emotions as determinants of intergroup attitudes. In D. M. Mackie & D. L. Hamilton (Eds.), *Affect, cognition, and stereotyping* (pp. 137–166). San Diego, CA: Academic Press.

Eugenical News. (1916–1922). *Monthly publication of the Eugenics Record Office*. Cold Springs, NY. Retrieved February 22, 2018, from https://babel.hathitrust.org/cgi/pt?id=coo.31924063788834.

Evans, W. S. (1931). *Organized eugenics*. New Haven, CT: American Eugenics Society.

Falkner, J., Schaller, M., Park, J. H., & Duncan, L. A. (2004). Evolved disease-avoidance mechanisms and contemporary xenophobic attitudes. *Group Processes & Intergroup Relations, 7*, 333–353.

Fanon, F. (1959/2008). *Black skin/White masks*. New York: Grove Press.

Fausto-Sterling, A. (1993). The five sexes. *The Sciences, 33*(2), 20–24.

Fernando, S. (1993). Racism and xenophobia. *Innovation: The European Journal of Social Sciences Research, 6*(1), 9–19.
Florack, A., Bless, H., & Piontkowski, U. (2003). When do people accept cultural diversity?: Affect as determinant. *International Journal of Intercultural Relations, 27*, 627–640.
Florack, A., Piontkowski, U., Rohmann, A., Balzer, T., & Perzig, S. (2003). Perceived intergroup threat and attitudes of host community members toward immigrant acculturation. *Journal of Social Psychology, 143*, 633–648.
Foner, N., & Fredrickson, G. M. (Eds.). (2004). *Not just Black and White: Historical and contemporary perspectives on immigration, race, and ethnicity in the United States*. New York: Russell Sage.
Freud, S. (1909). Analysis of a phobia in a five-year-old boy. In *The standard edition of the complete psychological works of Sigmund Freud, volume X (1909): Two case histories ('Little Hans' and the 'Rat Man')* (pp. 1–150). London: Hogarth Press.
Freud, S. (1930). *Civilization and its discontents* (Standard Edition). London: Hogarth Press.
Freud, S. (1953). *The standard edition of the complete psychological works of Sigmund Freud* (Trans. From the German by J. Strachey, A. Freud, & A. Richards). London: Hogarth Press.
Freud, S. (1964). *Complete psychological works of Sigmund Freud*. Standard edition. (Trans. by K. Strachey). London: Hogarth Press.
Friedman, H. (2009). Xenophilia as a cultural trap: Bridging the gap between transpersonal .... Retrieved from www.psycnet.apa.org/record/2012-07355-010.
Fritzsche, K. (1994). Conditions for xenophobia in eastern Germany (Formerly the GDR). In R. F. Farnen (Ed.), *Nationalism, ethnicity, and identity: Cross national and comparative perspectives* (pp. 277–284). Piscataway, NJ: Transaction Publishers.
Fromm, E. (1955). *The Sane Society*. Oxford, UK: Rinehart.
Frosh, S. (2004). Freud, psychoanalysis and anti-semitism. *Psychoanalytic Review, 91*(3), 309–330. https://doi.org/10.1521/prev.91.3.309.38302.
Fry, B. N. (2001). *Responding to immigration: Perceptions of promise and threat*. New York: LFB Scholarly Publishers.
Fuchs, L. H. (1995). The American civil culture and the inclusivist immigration policy. In J. A. Banks & C. A. McGee Banks (Eds.), *Handbook of research on multicultural education* (pp. 293–309). New York, NY: Macmillan.
Fuligni, A. J., Witkow, M., & Garcia, C. (2005). Ethnic identity and the academic adjustment of adolescents from Mexican, Chinese, and European backgrounds. *Developmental Psychology, 41*, 799–811.
Furnham, A. (1992). Relationship between knowledge of and attitudes towards AIDS. *Psychological Reports, 71*(3), 1149–1150.
Gabaccia, D. R. (2002). *Immigration and American diversity: A concise introduction*. Malden, MA: Blackwell.

Galton, F. (1865). Hereditary talent and character. *Macmillan's Magazine, 12*(157), 318–327.

Galton, F. (1869). *Hereditary genius: An inquiry into its laws and consequences.* New York: Macmillan.

Galton, F. (1883). *Inquiries into the human faculty & its development.* London: J.M. Dent.

Galton, F. (1904). Eugenics: Its definition, scope, and aims. *American Journal of Sociology, 10*(1), 1–25.

Gambino, C. P., Acosta, Y. D., & Grieco, E. M. (2014). *English-speaking ability of the foreign-born population in the United States: 2012.* American Community Service Reports, ACS-26. Washington, DC: U.S. Census Bureau.

Gellner, E. (1995). Nationalism and xenophobia. In B. Baumgartl & A. Favell (Eds.), *New xenophobia in Europe* (pp. 6–9). London: Kluwer Law International.

Gibson, R. K. (2002). *The growth of anti-immigrant parties in Western Europe.* Lewinston, NY: Edwin Mellen Press.

Gluszek, A., & Dovidio, J. F. (2010). Speaking with a nonnative accent: Perceptions of bias, communication difficulties, and belonging in the United States. *Journal of Language and Social Psychology, 29*(2), 224–234.

Goddard, H. H. (1911). The elimination of feeble-mindedness. *The Annals of the American Academy of Political and Social Science, 37*(2), 261–272.

Goddard, H. H. (1912). *The Kallikak family: A study in the heredity of feeble-mindedness.* New York: Macmillan.

Goddard, H. H. (1914). *Feeble-mindedness.* New York: Macmillan.

Goddard, H. H. (1917). Mental tests and the immigrant. *Journal of Delinquency, 2,* 243–277.

Goddard, H. H. (1919). *Psychology of the normal and subnormal.* New York: Dodd, Mead.

Gomez, A. (2016). *Another election surprise: Many Hispanics back Trump.* Retrieved from https://www.usatoday.com/story/news/politics/elections/2016/2016/11/09/hispanic-vote-election-2016-donald-trump-hillary-clinton/93540772/.

Goss, S., Wade, A., Skirvin, J. P., Morris, M., Bye, K. M., & Huston, D. (2013). *Effects of unauthorized immigration on the actuarial status of the social security trust funds.* Actuarial Note, 151. Baltimore, MD: Social Security Administration.

Gotanda, N. (1991). A critique of "our constitution is color-blind". *Stanford Law Review, 44,* 1–68.

Gottfredson, L. S. (2005). Suppressing intelligence research: Hurting those we intend to help. In R. H. Wright & N. A. Cummings (Eds.), *Destructive trends in mental health: The well-intentioned path to harm* (pp. 155–186). New York, NY: Routledge.

Gottfredson, L. S. (2012). Resolute ignorance on race and Rushton. *Personality and Individual Differences, 55,* 218–223. https://doi.org/10.1016/j.paid.2012.10.021.

Gould, S. J. (1995). *The mismeasure of man.* New York, NY: W.W. Norton & Company.

Gozdziak, E. M., & Collett, E. A. (2005). Research on human trafficking in North America: A review of literature. *International Migration, 43*(1–2), 99–128.

Grant, M. (1921). *The passing of the great race.* New York, NY: C. Scribner's Sons.

Gray, C. J. (1998). Cultivating citizenship through xenophobia in Gabon: 1960–1995. *Africa Today, 45,* 389–411.

Guia, A. (2016). The concept of nativism and anti-immigrant sentiments in Europe.*EUI Working Paper, MWP 2016/20.* San Domenico di Fiesoli, Italy: European University Institute. Retrieved on November 4, 2018, from http://cadmus.eui.eu/bitstream/handle/1814/43429/MWP_2016_20.pdf?sequence=1.

Guimond, S. (2000). Group socialization and prejudice: The social transmission of intergroup attitudes and beliefs. *European Journal of Social Psychology, 30,* 335–354.

Gur-Arie, R. (2014). American Eugenics Society (1926–1972). *Embryo Project Encyclopedia.* http://embryo.asu.edu/handle/10776/8241.

Hagendoorn, L., & Sniderman, P. (2001). Experimenting with a national sample: A Dutch survey of prejudice. *Patterns of Prejudice, 35,* 19–31.

Hall, G. S. (1881). *Aspects of German culture.* Boston: J.R. Osgood.

Hall, G. S. (1903). The white man's burden versus indigenous development of the lower races. *The Journal of Education, 58*(4, 1438), 83.

Hall, G. S. (1909). Evolution and psychology. In E. B. Poulton & G. S. Hall (Eds.), *Fifty years of Darwinism: Modern aspects of evolution* (pp. 251–267). Boston: H. Holt.

Hall, G. S. (1917a). *Jesus, the Christ, in the light of psychology.* New York: Doubleday, Page.

Hall, G. S. (1917b). Practical relations between psychology and the war. *Journal of Applied Psychology, 1*(1), 9–16. http://dx.doi.org/10.1037/h0070238.

Hannaford, I. (1996). *Race: The history of an idea in the West.* Washington, DC: Woodrow Wilson Center Press.

Hansen, K., Rakić, T., & Steffens, M. C. (2017). Foreign-looking native-accented people: More competent when first seen rather than heard. *Social Psychological and Personality Science.* https://doi.org/10.1177/1948550617732389.

Hatewatch. (2013). *Co-author of new immigration study says Latinos not as intelligent.* Retrieved from https://www.splcenter.org/hatewatch/2013/05/08/co-author-new-immigration-study-says-latinos-not-intelligent.

Haubert, J., & Fussell, E. (2006). Explaining pro-immigrant sentiment in the U.S.: Social class, cosmopolitanism, and perceptions of immigrants. *International Migration Review, 40,* 489–507.

Haynes, S. (2000). *Etruscan civilization: A cultural history.* Los Angeles, CA: Getty Publications.

Higham, J. (1988). *Strangers in the land.* New Brunswick, NJ: Rutgers University Press.

Head, K., & Ries, J. (1998). Immigration and trade creation: Econometric evidence from Canada. *Canadian Journal of Economics, 31,* 47–62.

Helms, J. E. (Ed.). (1990). *Black and White racial identity: Theory, research and practice.* Westport, CT: Greenwood.

Helms, J. E. (1994). The conceptualization of racial identity and other "racial" concepts. In E. Trickett, R. Watts, & D. Birman (Eds.), *Human diversity: Perspectives on people in context* (pp. 285–311). San Francisco: Jossey-Bass.

Helms, J. E., & Talleyrand, R. M. (1997). Race is not ethnicity. *American Psychologist, 52,* 1246–1247.

Hernandez, R. (1993, March 2). When an accent becomes an issue; Immigrants turn to speech classes to reduce sting of bias. *New York Times,* New York City. Retrieved March 20, 2012, from http://www.nytimes.com/1993/03/02/nyregion/when-accent-becomes-issueimmigrants-turn-speech-classes-reduce-sting-bias.html?pagewanted=all&src=pm.

Ho, R. (1987). Immigrants and immigration: A survey of attitudes. *Australian Psychologist, 22,* 3–16.

Hofstra, J., Van Oudenhoven, J. P., & Buunk, B. P. (2005). Attachment styles and majority members' attitudes towards adaptation strategies of immigrants. *International Journal of Intercultural Relations, 29,* 601–619.

Horenczyk, G. (1996). Immigrants' perceptions of host attitudes and their reconstruction of cultural groups. *Applied Psychology: An International Review, 46,* 34–38.

Hosoda, M., & Stone-Romero, E. (2010). The effects of foreign accents on employment-related decisions. *Journal of Managerial Psychology, 25,* 113–132. https://doi.org/10.1108/02683941011019339.

Hovey, J. D. (2000). Acculturative stress, depression, and suicidal ideation in Mexican immigrants. *Cultural Diversity and Ethnic Minority Psychology, 6,* 134–151.

Hovey, J. D., & Magana, C. J. (2003). Psychosocial predictors of anxiety among immigrant Mexican migrant farmworkers: Implications for prevention and treatment. *Cultural Diversity and Ethnic Minority Psychology, 8,* 274–289.

Hovey, J. D., Rojas, R. S., Kain, C., & Magaña, C. (2000). Proposition 187 reexamined: Attitudes toward immigration among California voters. *Current Psychology: Developmental, Learning, Personality, Social, 19,* 159–174.

Ioanide, P. (2014). The alchemy of race and affect: "White innocence" and public secrets in the post-civil rights era. *Kalfou, 1*(1), 151–168.

Jasinskaja-Lahti, I., Liebkind, K., & Perhoniemi, R. (2006). Perceived discrimination and well-being: A victim study of different immigrant groups. *Journal of Community and Applied Social Psychology, 16*, 267–284.

Jasinskaja-Lahti, I., Liebkind, K., Jaakkola, M., & Reuter, A. (2006). Perceived discrimination, social support networks, and psychological well-being among three immigrant groups. *Journal of Cross-Cultural Psychology, 37*, 293–311.

Jaynes, G. D. (Ed.). (2000). *Immigration and race: New challenges for American democracy*. New Haven, CT: Yale University Press.

Johnson, G. E. (1980). The labor market effects of immigration. *Illinois Law Review, 33*(3), 331–341.

Jones, K. W. (2001). *Accent on privilege: English identities and Anglophilia in the US*. Philadelphia, PA: Temple University Press.

Jost, J. T., & Banaji, M. R. (1994). The role of stereotyping in system-justification and he production of false consciousness. *British Journal of Social Psychology, 33*, 1–27.

Jost, J. T., Banaji, M. R., & Nosek, B. A. (2004). A decade of system justification theory: Accumulated evidence of conscious and unconscious bolstering of the status quo. *Political Psychology, 25*(6), 881–919.

Jung, Y. (2004). Can Japan become a "society attractive to immigrants?": Identity, gender, and nation-states under globalization in East Asia. *International Journal of Japanese Sociology, 13*, 53–68.

Kam, C. D., & Kinder, D. R. (2007). Terror and ethnocentrism: Foundations of American support for the war on terrorism. *The Journal of Politics, 69*(2), 320–338.

Kanazawa, S., & Frerichs, R. L. (2001). Why single men might abhor foreign cultures. *Social Biology, 48*, 321–328.

Katz, J. (1980). *From prejudice to destruction: Anti-semitism, 1700–1933*. Cambridge, UK: Harvard University Press.

Katz, I., Wachenhut, J., & Haas, R. G. (1986). Racial ambivalence, value duality, and behavior. In J. F. Dovidio & S. L. Gaertner (Eds.), *Prejudice, discrimination, and racism* (pp. 35–60). New York: Academic Press.

Kim, C. J. (2000). *Bitter fruit: The politics of Black-Korean conflict in New York City*. New Haven, CT: Yale University Press.

Kivisto, P., & Faist, T. (2009). *Beyond a border: The causes and consequences of contemporary immigration*. Thousand Oaks, CA: Sage.

Klotz, A. (2000). Migration after the apartheid: Deracializing South African policy. *Third World Quarterly, 21*, 831–847.

Korte, G., & Gomez, A. (2018, May 16). Trump ramps up rhetoric on undocumented immigrants: 'These aren't people. These are animals'. *The USA Today*. Retrieved from https://www.usatoday.com/story/news/politics/2018/05/16/trump-immigrants-animals-mexico-democrats-sanctuary-cities/617252002/.

Kosic, A., Mannetti, L., & Sam, D. L. (2005). The role of majority attitudes towards out-group in the perception of the acculturation strategies of immigrants. *International Journal of Intercultural Relations, 29*, 273–288.

Kramer, H., & Sprenger, J. (1486). *The Malleus Maleficarum of Heinrich Kramer and James Sprenger* (W. Lovelace & C. Rice, Trans. [1928/1948]).

Kropotkin, P. (1914/2012). *Mutual aid: A factor of evolution*. Mineola, NY: Dover.

Kuhl, S. (2002). *The Nazi connection: Eugenics, American racism, and German national socialism*. New York: Oxford University Press.

Kurman, J., Eshel, Y., & Sbeit, K. (2005). Acculturation attitudes, perceived attitudes of the majority, and adjustment of Israeli-Arab and Jewish-Ethiopian students to an Israeli university. *Journal of Social Psychology, 145*, 593–612.

Lacan, J. (1978/1998). *The four fundamental concepts of psycho-analysis*. New York, NY: W.W. Norton & Company.

Larsen, L. J. (2004). *The foreign-born population in the United States: 2003*. Current Population Reports, P20-551. Washington, DC: U.S. Census Bureau.

Layton, L. (2002). Cultural hierarchies, splitting and the hetrosexist unconscious. In S. Fairfield, L. Layton, & C. Stack (Eds.), *Bringing the plague: Toward a postmodern psychoanalysis* (pp. 195–223). New York: Other Press.

Layton, L. (2009). Who's responsible? Our mutual implication in each other's suffering. *Psychoanalytic Dialogues, 19*(2), 105–120.

Layton, L. (2010). Irrational exuberance: Neoliberal subjectivity and the perversion of truth. *Subjectivity, 3*(3), 303–322.

Lazarus, E. (1883). The new colossus. *A Century of Immigration, 1820–1924*. Library of Congress. Retrieved from https://memory.loc.gov/ammem/awhhtml/awlaw3/immigration.html.

Le Espiritu, Y. (2003). *Home bound: Filipino American lives across cultures, communities, and countries*. Berkeley, CA: University of California Press.

Lee, R. G. (2003). *Orientals: Asian American in popular culture*. Philadelphia, PA: Temple University Press.

Lee, M. T., & Martinez, R. (2009). Immigration reduces crime: An emerging scholarly consensus. In *Immigration, crime and justice* (pp. 3–16). Bingley, UK: Emerald Group Publishing Limited.

Lee, M. T., Martinez, R., & Rosenfeld, R. (2001). Does immigration increase homicide? Negative evidence from three border cities. *Sociological Quarterly, 42*, 559–580.

LeMay, M. C. (2004). *U.S. immigration: A reference handbook*. Santa Barbara, CA: ABC CLIO.

Lemish, D. (2001). The whore and the other: Israeli images of female immigrants from the former USSR. *Gender & Society, 14*, 333–349.

Leonhardt, D. (2007). Truth, fiction, and Lou Dobbs. *The New York Times*. Retrieved November 2, 2018 from https://www.nytimes.com/2007/05/30/business/30leonhardt.html.

Lerner, M. (1980). *The belief in a just world: A fundamental delusion*. New York, NY: Plenum Press.

Lev-Ari, S., & Keysar, B. (2010). Why don't we believe nonnative speakers? The influence of accent on credibility. *Journal of Experimental Social Psychology, 46*, 1093–1096. https://doi.org/10.1016/j.jesp.2010.05.02.

Levinas, E. (1996). *Emmanuel Levinas: Basic philosophical writings*. Bloomington, IN: Indiana University Press.

LeVine, R. A., & Campbell, D. T. (1972). *Ethnocentrism: Theories of conflict, ethnic attitudes, and group behavior*. New York: Wiley.

Licata, L., & Klein, O. (2002). Does European citizenship breed xenophobia?: European identification as a predictor of intolerance towards immigrants. *Journal of Community and Applied Social Psychology, 12*, 323–337.

Liebkind, K., & Jasinskaja-Lahti, I. (2000). The influence of experiences of discrimination on psychological stress: A comparison of seven immigrant groups. *Journal of Community and Applied Social Psychology, 10*, 1–16.

Liebkind, K., Jasinskaja-Lahti, I., & Solheim, E. (2004). Cultural identity, perceived discrimination, and parental support as determinants of immigrants' school adjustment: Vietnamese youth in Finland. *Journal of Adolescent Research, 19*, 635–656.

Lin, A. C., & Green, N. W. (2001). *Immigration*. Washington, DC: Division of Congressional Quarterly.

Linthicum, K. (2015). *Group says California immigration policies contribute to drought*. Retrieved from http://www.latimes.com/local/california/la-me-immigration-drought-20150524-story.html.

Lipsitz, G. (2006). *The possessive investment in whiteness: How white people profit from identity politics*. Philadelphia, PA: Temple University Press.

Lombardo, P. A. (Ed.). (2011). *A century of eugenics in America: From the Indiana experiment to the human genome era*. Bloomington, IN: Indiana University Press.

Longoria, T. (1996). White attitudes toward minority electoral districts: Minority population size, national politics, and local policy. *Social Science Quarterly, 77*, 877–887.

Lopez, G., & Radford, J. (2017). *Facts on U.S. immigrants, 2015*. Pew Research Center Reports. Retrieved June 18, 2018, from http://www.pewhispanic.org/2017/05/03/facts-on-u-s-immigrants/#2013-fb-authorized-pie.

Lorenz, H. S., & Watkins, M. (2001). Silenced knowings, forgotten springs: Paths to healing in the wake of colonialism. *Radical Psychology, 2*(2), 1–19.

Lovelace, W. (1928/2002). *Introduction to Malleus Maleficarum*. Online HTML Scripting Copyright © 1998–2001 by the Windhaven Network, Inc.

Lynn, R. (2001). *Eugenics: A reassessment*. New York: Praeger.

Lyons, P. D., & Clark, J. J. (2008). Interaction, enculturation, social distance, and ancient ethnic identities. In L. D. Webster, M. E. McBrinn, & E. Gamboa Carrera (Eds.), *Archaeology without borders: Contact, commerce, and change in the US Southwest and Northwestern Mexico* (pp. 185–207). Boulder: University Press of Colorado.

MacDonald, K. (1998). *Separation and its discontents: Toward an evolutionary theory of anti-semitism*. Westport, CT: Praeger.

MacDonald, K. (2005). Personality, evolution, and development. Evolutionary perspectives on human development. In R. L. Burgess, R. G. Burgess, & K. MacDonald (Eds.), *Evolutionary perspectives on human development* (pp. 207–242). Thousand Oaks, CA: Sage.

Marger, N. (1997). *Race and ethnic relations: American and global perspective*. New York: International Thompson Publishing.

Marks, G. N. (2005). Accounting for immigrant non-immigrant differences in reading and mathematics in twenty countries. *Ethnic and Racial Studies, 28*(5), 925–946.

Marsella, A. J., & Ring, E. (2003). Human migration and immigration: An overview. In L. L. Adler & U. P. Gielen (Eds.), *Migration: Immigration and emigration in international perspective* (pp. 3–22). Westport, CT: Praeger.

McClintock, A. (1995). *Imperial leather: Race, gender and sexuality in the colonial contest*. New York: Routledge.

McDougall, W. (1921). *National welfare and national decay*. London: Methuen & Co. Ltd.

McKinnon, S. (2005). *Neo-liberal genetics: The myths and moral tales of evolutionary psychology*. Chicago, IL: Prickly Paradigm Press.

McKinnon, S., & Silverman, S. (Eds.). (2005). *Complexities: Beyond nature and nurture*. Chicago, IL: University of Chicago Press.

Memmi, A. (2013). *The colonizer and the colonized*. New York: Routledge.

Mercer, K. (1993). Reading racial fetishism: The photographs of Robert Mapplethorpe. In E. Apter & W. Pietz (Eds.), *Fetishism as cultural discourse*. Ithaca: Cornell University Press.

Merriam Webster. (2018). *History of xenophobia*. Retrieved from https://www.merriam-webster.com/words-at-play/a-short-history-of-xenophobia.

Merskin, D. L. (2011). *Media, minorities, and meaning: A critical introduction*. New York: Peter Lang.

Miles, R. (1982). *Racism and migrant labour: A critical text*. London: Routledge.

Mills, N. (Ed.). (1994). *Arguing immigration: Are new immigrants a wealth of diversity… or a crushing burden?* New York: Simon & Schuster.

Misago, J. P., Freemantle, I., & Landau, L. B. (2015). *Protection from xenophobia: An evaluation of UNHCR's regional office for Southern Africa's xenophobia related programmes*. Witwatersrand, South Africa: The African Center for Migration and Society. Retrieved from http://www.unhcr.org/55cb153f9.pdf.

Moradi, B., & Hasan, N. T. (2004). Arab American persons' reported experiences of discrimination and mental health: The mediating role of personal control. *Journal of Counseling Psychology, 51*, 418–428.

Morrison, T. (1994). On the backs of blacks. In N. Mills (Ed.), *Arguing immigration: Are new immigrants a wealth of diversity… or a crushing burden?* (pp. 97–100). New York: Simon & Schuster.

Mugny, G., Kaiser, C., Papastamou, S., & Pérez, J. A. (1984). Intergroup relations, identification, and social influence. *British Journal of Social Psychology, 23*, 317–322.

Mugny, G., Sanchez-Mazas, M., Roux, P., & Pérez, J. A. (1991). Independence and interdependence of group judgments: Xenophobia and minority influence. *European Journal of Social Psychology, 21*, 213–223.

Mulder, T. J., Hollmann, F. W., Lollock, L. R., Cassidy, R. C., Costanzo, J. M., & Baker, J. D. (2001). *U.S. Census Bureau measurement of net international migration to the United States: 1990–2000.* Washington, DC: Population Division U.S. Census Bureau. http://www.census.gov/population.

Muller, T., & Espanshade, T. J. (1985). *The fourth wave: California's newest immigrants.* Washington, DC: Urban Institute.

Munro, N. (2006). The immigrant numbers game. *National Journal, 38*, 5–7.

Navas, M. S. (1998). New measurement instruments for the new racism. *Revista de Psiocologia Social, 13*, 233–239.

National Genome Research Association. (2006). *Whole genome association studies.* Retrieved from https://www.genome.gov/17516714/2006-release-about-whole-genome-association-studies/.

Ng, S. H. (2007). Language-based discrimination: Blatant and subtle forms. *Journal of Language and Social Psychology, 26*, 106–122. https://doi.org/10.1177/0261927X07300074.

Norrasteh, A. (2016). *Terrorism and immigration: Risk analysis.* The CATO Institute, Policy Analysis No. 798. Retrieved June 18, 2018, from https://www.cato.org/publications/policy-analysis/terrorism-immigration-risk-analysis.

Oakley, R. (1996). *Tackling racist and xenophobic violence in Europe: Review and practical guidelines.* Strasbourg, Germany: Council of Europe Publishing.

Ochoa, G. L. (2000). Mexican Americans' attitudes toward and interactions with Mexican immigrants: A qualitative analysis of conflict and cooperation. *Social Science Quarterly, 81*, 84–105.

Ommundsen, R., & Larsen, K. S. (1997). Attitudes toward illegal aliens: The reliability and validity of a Likert-type scale. *Journal of Social Psychology, 137*, 665–667.

Ommundsen, R., Van der Veer, K., Yakushko, O., & Ullenberg, P. (2013). Exploring the relationships between fear-based xenophobia, social contact, and perceptions of out-group entitativity in Norway. *Psychological Reports, 112*(1), 109–124.

Ortega, F., & Peri, G. (2009). *The causes and effects of international migrations: Evidence from OECD countries 1980–2005* (No. W14833). National Bureau of Economic Research.

Ott, E. M. (1995). Effects of the male female ration at work: Policewomen and male nurses. *Psychology of Women Quarterly, 13,* 41–57.

Ousey, G. C., & Kubrin, C. E. (2009). Exploring the connection between immigration and violent crime rates in U.S. cities, 1980–2000. *Social Problems, 56*(3), 447–473.

Padilla, A. M., & Perez, W. (2003). Acculturation, social identity, and social cognition: A new perspective. *Hispanic Journal of Behavioral Sciences, 25,* 35–55.

Passel, J. S. (2006). *Size and characteristics of the unauthorized migrant population in the U.S.: Estimates based on the March 2005 current population survey.* Pew Hispanic Center. Retrieved August 28, 2006, from http://pewhispanic.org/reports/report.php?ReportID=61.

Patterson, O. (1982). *Slavery and social death.* Cambridge, MA: Harvard University Press.

Pearson, K. (1905). *National life from the standpoint of science.* London: Adam and Black.

Pearson, K. (1911). *The scope and importance to the state of the science of national eugenics.* London: Dulau and Company.

Pearson, K. (1930). *The life, letters and labours of Francis Galton.* Cambridge, UK: Cambridge University Press.

Pedahzur, A., & Yishai, Y. (1999). Hatred by hated people: Xenophobia in Israel. *Studies in Conflict & Terrorism, 22,* 101–117.

Perea, J. F. (1997). Introduction. In J. F. Perea (Ed.), *Immigrants out! The new nativism and the anti-immigrant impulse in the United States* (pp. 1–12). New York: New York University Press.

Perry, M., Vandervate, B., Auman, L., & Morris, K. (2001). *Evaluating components of international migration: Legal migrants* (Population Division Working Paper #59), Washington, DC: U.S. Government. Retrieved July 16, 2002, from http://www.census.gov/population.

Pettigrew, T. F. (1998). Reactions toward the new minorities of Western Europe. *Annual Review of Sociology, 24,* 77–103.

Pew Hispanic Center. (2006, May 22). *Modes of entry for the unauthorized migrant population.* Retrieved January 3, 2007, from http://pewhispanic.org/files/factsheets/19.pdf.

Pew Hispanic Center. (2016). *Occupations of unauthorized immigrants.* Retrieved from http://www.pewhispanic.org/2016/11/03/occupations-of-unauthorized-immigrant-workers/.

Pinker, S. (2002). *The blank slate: The modern denial of human nature.* New York, NY: Penguin.

Pinker, S. (2005). Sex ed. *The New Republic.* Retrieved May 18, 2018, from https://newrepublic.com/article/68044/sex-ed.

Pinker, S. (2011). *The better angels of our nature: The decline of violence in history and its causes.* London, UK: Penguin.

Pinker, S. (2018). *Enlightenment now: The case for reason, science, humanism, and progress*. New York: Penguin.

Pioneer Fund. (2013). Website archived at https://web.archive.org/web/20130412144849/http://www.pioneerfund.org/.

Pittinsky, T. L., Rosenthal, S. A., & Montoya, R. M. (2010). Measuring positive attitudes toward outgroups: Development and validation of the allophilia scale. In L. Tropp & R. Mallett (Eds.), *Beyond prejudice reduction: Pathways to positive intergroup relations*. Washington, DC: American Psychological Association.

Poole, E., & Richardson, J. E. (Eds.). (2010). *Muslims and the news media*. London, UK: I.B. Tauris.

Popenoe, P., & Johnson, R. H. (1918/1935). *Applied eugenics*. New York: Macmillan.

Pratt, G. (1999). From registered nurse to registered nanny: Discursive geographies of Filipina domestic workers in Vancouver, BC. *Economic Geography, 75,* 215–236.

Pratt, M. L. (1991). Arts of the contact zone. *Profession, 91*, 33–40.

Pratto, F., & Lemieux, A. F. (2001). The psychological ambiguity of immigration and its implications for promoting immigration policy. *Journal of Social Issues, 57,* 413–430.

Pratto, F., Sidanius, J., Stallworth, L. M., & Malle, B. F. (1994). Social dominance orientation: A personality variable predicting social and political attitudes. *Journal of Personality and Social Psychology, 67,* 741–763.

Prillrltensky, I., & Nelson, G. (2002). *Doing psychology critically: Making a difference in diverse settings*. New York: Palgrave Macmillan.

Pritzker, B. (2000). *A native American encyclopedia: History, culture, and peoples*. New York, NY: Oxford University Press.

Quillian, L. (1995). Prejudice as a response to perceived group threat: Population composition and anti-immigrant and racial prejudice in Europe. *American Sociological Review, 60,* 585–611.

Radkiewicz, P. (2003). The national values as a concept helpful in explaining the development of nationalistic attitudes and xenophobia. *Polish Psychological Bulletin, 34,* 5–13.

Rakić, T., Steffens, M. C., & Mummendey, A. (2011). Blinded by the accent! The minor role of looks in ethnic categorization. *Journal of Personality and Social Psychology, 100,* 16–29. https://doi.org/10.1037/a0021522.

Remennick, L. (2005). Immigration, gender, and psychosocial adjustment: A study of 150 immigrant couples in Israel. *Sex Roles, 53*(11–12), 847–863.

Reynolds, V., & Vine, I. (1987). *The socio-biology of ethnocentrism: Evolutionary dimensions of xenophobia, discrimination, racism, and nationalism*. London: Croom Helm.

Roosevelt, T. (1894, April). True Americanism. *The Forum Magazine*, p. 3.

Runciman, W. G. (1966). *Relative deprivation and social justice: A study of attitudes to social inequality in twentieth-century England*. Berkeley: University of California Press.

Rushton, P. (2000). Speech at the American renaissance conference. Quote retrieved from Southern Poverty Law Center website at https://www.splcenter.org/fighting-hate/extremist-files/individual/jean-philipperushton.

Rushton, J. P. (1990). Sir Francis Galton, epigenetic rules, genetic similarity theory, and human life-history analysis. *Journal of Personality, 58*(1), 117–140.

Rushton, J. P. (1995). *Race, evolution, and behavior*. New Brunswick, NJ: Transaction Publishers.

Rushton, J. P. (1999). Genetic similarity theory and the nature of ethnocentrism. In K. Thienpont & R. Cliquet (Eds.), *In-group/out-group behavior in modern societies: An evolutionary perspective*. Amsterdam, The Netherlands: Vlaamse Gemeeschap/CBGS.

Rushton, J. P. (2005). Ethnic nationalism, evolutionary psychology and genetic similarity theory. *Nations and Nationalism, 11*(4), 489–507.

Rushton, J. P., & Jensen, A. R. (2005). Wanted: More race realism, less moralistic fallacy. *Psychology, Public Policy, and Law, 11*(2), 328–336. https://doi.org/10.1037/1076-8971.11.2.328.

Ruti, M. (2015). *The age of scientific sexism: How evolutionary psychology promotes gender profiling and fans the battle of the sexes*. Toronto, ON, Canada: Bloomsbury Publishing.

Rydgren, J. (2004). The logic of xenophobia. *Rationality and Society, 16*, 123–148.

Said, E. W. (1983). *The world, the text, and the critic*. Cambridge, MA: Harvard University Press.

Said, E. (1993). The politics of knowledge. In C. McCarthy & W. Crichlow (Eds.), *Race, identify and representation in education* (pp. 306–314). New York: Routledge.

Saleeby, C. W. (1911). *Woman and womanhood: A search for principles*. New York: Kennerley.

Sam, D. L. (1995). Acculturation attitudes among young immigrants as a function of perceived parental attitudes toward cultural change. *Journal of Early Adolescence, 15*(2), 238–258.

Sanchez-Mazas, M. (1996). Minority influence under value conflict: The case of human rights and xenophobia. *British Journal of Social Psychology, 35*, 169–178.

Sanger, M. (1919, February). Birth control and racial betterment. *Eugenical News*.

Sanger, M. (1921). The eugenic value of birth control propaganda. *Birth Control Review, 5*(10), 1–10.

Sartre, J. P. (1943/1956). *Being and Nothingness* (Trans. by Hazel E. Barnes). New York, NY: Philosophical Library.

Schirmer, D. (1998). Introduction. In N. Finzsch & D. Schirmer (Eds.), *Identity and intolerance: Nationalism, racism, and xenophobia in Germany and the United States* (pp. xi–xxxix). Washington, DC: Cambridge University Press.

Schultz, E. (2016). Bhutanese refugee crisis: A brief history. *The Seattle Times*. Retrieved from https://www.seattletimes.com/seattle-news/bhutanese-refugee-crisis-a-brief-history/.

Seely, M. (2012). *Born expecting the pleistocene: Psychology and the problem of civilization*. Cobham, UK: Old Dog books.

Segura, D. A. (1989). Chicana and Mexican immigrant women at work: The impact of class, race, and gender on occupational mobility. *Gender & Society, 3*(1), 37–52.

Selden, S. (1999). *Inheriting shame: The story of eugenics and racism in America*. New York: Teachers College Press.

Shelley, L. (2010). *Human trafficking: A global perspective*. Cambridge, MA: Cambridge University Press.

Shiochet, C. E. (2015). Immigrants and crime: Crunching the numbers. *CNN Reports*. Retrieved June 18, 2018, from https://www.cnn.com/2015/07/08/politics/immigrants-crime/.

Sen, A. (1994). *Population: Delusion and reality*. Lecture delivered at the United Nations on April 18, 1994 for the Eminent Citizens Committee for Cairo '94 conference.

Shamai, S., & Ilatov, Z. (2001). Assimilation and ethnic boundaries: Israeli students' attitudes toward Soviet immigrants. *Adolescence, 36*, 681–695.

Sheunpflug, A. (1997). Cross-cultural encounters as a way to reduce xenophobia. *International Education Review, 43*, 109–116.

Sherif, M., Harvey, O. J., White, B. J., Hood, W. R., & Sherif, C. W. (1961). *Intergroup cooperation and conflict: The robbers cave experiment*. Norman, OK: University of Oklahoma Book Exchange.

Silva, E. B. (2003). *Racism without racists: Color-blind racism and the persistence of racial inequality in the United States*. Lanham, MD: Rowman & Littlefield.

Silva, C. (2018). Trump's full list of 'racist' comments about immigrants, Muslims and others. *The Newsweek*. Retrieved from https://www.newsweek.com/trumps-full-list-racist-comments-about-immigrants-muslims-and-others-779061.

Simon, R. J. (Ed.). (2001). *Immigrant women*. New Brunswick: Transaction Publishers.

Sloan, T. (2005). Globalization, poverty, and social justice. In G. Nelson & I. Prilleltensky (Eds.), *Community psychology: In pursuit of liberation and well-being* (pp. 309–329). New York: Palgrave.

Smelser, N. J., & Baltes, P. B. (Eds.). (2001). *International encyclopedia of the social and behavioural sciences*. Oxford: Oxford Science Ltd./Elsevier.

Smith, J. D. (1985). *Minds made feeble: The myth and legacy of the Kallikaks*. Rockville, MD: Aspen.

Smith, J. P., & Edmonston, B. (1997). *The new Americans: Economic, demographic, and fiscal effects of immigration*. Washington, DC: National Academy Press.

Social Biology. (1973). A new name society for the study of social biology (Formerly the American Eugenics Society). *Social Biology, 20*(1), 1. https://doi.org/10.1080/19485565.1973.9988017.

Solnit, R. (2004). The Siege of the Sierra Club anti-immigration ideologues must not be allowed to hijack John Muir's vision. *Mother Jones*. Retrieved from https://www.motherjones.com/environment/2004/03/siege-sierra-club/.

Sorensen, M., & Krahn, H. (1996). Attitudes toward immigrants: A test of two theories. *Alberta Journal of Educational Research, 42*, 3–18.

Southern Poverty Law Center. (2017). *The Pioneer Fund*. Retrieved on November 2, 2018, from https://www.splcenter.org/fighting-hate/extremist-files/group/pioneer-fund.

Southern Poverty Law Center. (2018). *Jean-Philippe Rushton*. Retrieved on November 2, 2018, from https://www.splcenter.org/fighting-hate/extremist-files/individual/jean-philippe-rushton.

Spivak, G. (2013). *The Spivak reader: Selected works of Gayati Chakravorty Spivak*. London, UK: Routledge.

Steele, S. (1990). White guilt. *American Scholar, 59*, 497–506.

Stein, G. J. (2002). From passive periphery to active agents: Emerging perspectives in the archaeology of interregional interaction. *American Anthropologist, 104*(3), 903–916.

Steiner, E. A. (1909). *The immigrant tide: Its ebb and flow*. New York: F.H. Revell.

Stephan, W. G., Renfro, C. L., Esses, V. M., Stephan, C. W., & Martin, T. (2005). The effects of feeling threatened on attitudes toward immigrants. *International Journal of Intercultural Relations, 29*, 1–19.

Stephan, W. G., & Stephan, C. W. (1996). *Intergroup relations*. Boulder, CO: Westview Press.

Stephan, C. W., & Stephan, W. S. (2013). An integrated threat theory of prejudice. In S. Oskamp (Ed.). *Reducing prejudice and discrimination* (pp. 33–56). New York: Psychology Press.

Stephan, W. G., Ybarra, O., & Bachman, G. (1999). Prejudice toward immigrants: An integrated threat theory. *Journal of Applied Social Psychology, 29*, 2221–2237.

Stephan, W. G., Ybarra, O., Martinez, C., Scharzwald, J., & Tur-Kaspa, D. (1998). Prejudice toward immigrants to Spain and Israel: An integrated threat theory analysis. *Journal of Cross-Cultural Psychology, 29*, 559–576.

Streeck-Fischer, A. (1999). Xenophobia and violence by adolescent skin-heads. In M. Sugar, (Ed.), *Trauma and adolescence.* Monograph Series of the International Society for Adolescent Psychiatry (Vol. 1, pp. 251–269). Madison: International Universities Press.

Stürmer, S. (2013). *Psychological foundations of xenophilia: The role of major personality.* Retrieved from https://www.ncbi.nlm.nih.gov/pubmed/23834640.

Suarez-Orozco, C., & Suarez-Orozco, M. (1995). *Transformations: Immigration, family life, and achievement motivation among Latino adolescents.* Palo Alto: Stanford University Press.

Sue, D. W. (2003). *Overcoming our racism: The journey to liberation.* New York: John Wiley & Sons.

Tactaquin, C. (1998). The greening of the anti-immigrant agenda. *Network News*, Spring Issue.

Taggart, P. (2000). *Populism.* Buckingham: Open University Press.

Takaki, R. (1989). *Strangers from a different shore.* Boston, MA: Little Brown.

Taras, R. (2012). *Xenophobia and Islamophobia in Europe.* Edinburgh, UK: Edinburgh University Press.

Tatum, B. D. (1994). Teaching White students about racism: The search for White allies and the restoration of hope. *Teacher College Record, 95*, 462–476.

Taylor, M. C. (1998). How Whites attitudes vary with the racial composition of local populations: Number count. *American Sociological Review, 63*, 512–535.

Teaching Tolerance. (2011). *Ten myths about immigration.* Issues 39. Retrieved June 25, 2018, from https://www.tolerance.org/magazine/spring-2011/ten-myths-about-immigration.

Terman, L. M. (1916). *The measurement of intelligence.* New York: Houghton Mifflin.

The Institute for Women's Policy Research. (2018). *Immigrant women.* Retrieved June 19, 2018, from https://statusofwomendata.org/immigrant-women/.

Thornton, M. C., & Mizuno, Y. (1999). Economic well-being and Black adult feelings toward immigrants and Whites, 1984. *Journal of Black Studies, 30*, 15–44.

Tougas, F., De La Sablonnière, R., Lagacé, M., & Kocum, L. (2003). Intrusiveness of minorities: Growing pains for the majority group? *Journal of Applied Social Psychology, 33*, 283–298.

Tucker, W. H. (1996). *The science and politics of racial research.* Urbana-Champaign: University of Illinois Press.

Unger, R. K., & Crawford, M. E. (1992). *Women and gender: A feminist psychology.* Philadelphia: Temple University Press.

UNHCR. (2001). *International migration, racism, discrimination and xenophobia*. A Publication Jointly Produced by the International Labor Organization, International Organization for Migration, and the Office of the United Nations High Commisioner for Human Rights. Geneva, Switzerland: The UN Nigh Commissioner for Refugees. Retrieved November 2, 2018, from https://www2.ohchr.org/english/issues/migration/taskforce/docs/wcar.pdf.

UNHCR. (2009). *Protection from xenophobia*. http://www.unhcr.org/55cb153f9.pdf.

UNHCR. (2018). *Refugee crisis in Europe*. Office of Emergencies, the United Nations. Retrieved from https://www.unrefugees.org/emergencies/refugee-crisis-in-europe/.

United Nations. (2006). *State of the world's refugees, 2006*. Retrieved August 28, 2006, from http://www.unhcr.org/cgi-bin/texis/vtx/template?page=publ&src=static/sowr2006/toceng.htm.

U.S. Citizen and Immigration Services. (2018). *Green Card eligibility categories*. https://www.uscis.gov/greencard/eligibility-categories.

U.S. Congress. (2004). *Mail-order bride business*. U.S. Legal Code, Title 8, Chapter 12, Subchapter II, Part IX, § 1375. Retrieved August 16, 2006, from http://www4.law.cornell.edu/uscode/html/uscode08/usc_sec08_00001375-000-.html.

U.S. Department of State. (2005). *Trafficking in persons report, 2005*. Retrieved August 16, 2006, from http://www.state.gov/g/tip/rls/tiprpt/2005.

Vale, P. (2002). Migration, xenophobia, and security-making in post-apartheid South Africa. *Politikon, 29*, 7–29.

van den Berghe, P. L. (1999). Racism, ethnocentrism, and xenophobia: In our genes or in our memes? In K. Thienpont & R. Cliquet (Eds.), *In-group/out-group behavior in modern societies*. Amsterdam, The Netherlands: NIDI CBGS Publications.

van der Dennen, J. M. G. (1987). Ethnocentrism and in-group/out-group differentiation: A review and interpretation of the literature. In V. Reynolds, V. S. E. Falger, & I. Vine (Eds.), *The sociobiology of ethnocentrism: Evolutionary dimensions of xenophobia, discrimination, racism, and nationalism* (pp. 1–47). London: Croom Helm.

Van der Veer, K., Ommundsen, R., Yakushko, O., & Higler, L. (2011). Cross-national measure of fear-based xenophobia: Development of a cumulative scale. *Psychological Reports, 109*(1), 27–42. https://doi.org/10.2466/07.17.pro.109.4.

Van der Veer, K., Ommundsen, R., Yakushko, O., Higler, L., Woelders, S., & Hagen, K. A. (2013). Psychometrically and qualitatively validating a cross-national cumulative measure of fear-based xenophobia. *Quality and Quantity in Psychology, 47*, 1423–1444.

Waldinger, R. (1997). Black/immigrant competition re-assessed: New evidence from Los Angeles. *Sociological Perspectives, 40,* 365–386.

Waldinger, R., Ward, R., & Aldrich, H. (1985). Ethnic business and occupational mobility in advanced societies. *Sociology, 19*(4), 586–597.

Washburn, M. F. (1923). A questionary study of certain national differences in emotional traits. *Journal of Comparative Psychology, 3*(6), 413–430.

Washington, J. (2018, June 27). Here is just some of the hateful abuse immigrants face in detention centers. *The Nation.* Retrieved June 19, 2018, from https://www.thenation.com/article/just-hateful-abuse-immigrants-face-detention-centers/.

Watson, J. B. (1914). *Behavior: An introduction to comparative psychology.* New York: H. Holt.

Watson, J. B. (1919). *Psychology: From the standpoint of a behaviorist.* New York: Lippincott.

Watson, J. B. (1928). *Psychological care of infant and child.* New York: W.W. Norton.

Watts, M. W. (1996). Political xenophobia in the transition from socialism: Threat, racism and ideology among East German youth. *Political Psychology, 17,* 97–126.

Weikart, R. (2004). *From Darwin to Hitler: Evolutionary ethics, eugenics, and racism in Germany.* New York: Palgrave Macmillan.

Wiggam, A. E. (1923). *The new decalogue of science.* Indianapolis, IN: Bobbs-Merrill.

Williamson, J. (1997). Globalization and inequality, past and present. *The World Bank Research Observer, 12,* 117–135.

Wilson, E. O. (1975). *Sociobiology: The new synthesis.* Cambridge, MA: Harvard University Press.

Wimmer, A. (1997). Explaining xenophobia and racism: A critical review of current research approaches. *Ethnic and Racial Studies, 20,* 17–41.

Wistrich, R. S. (1999). The devil, the Jews and hatred of the "other." In R. S. Wistrich (Ed.), *Demonizing the other.* Amsterdam, NL: Harwood Academic.

Wistrich, R. S. (2011). *Demonizing the other: Antisemitism, racism, and xenophobia.* London, UK: Routledge.

Wolfram, W., & Schilling-Estes, N. (2006). *American English: Dialects and variation* (2nd ed.). Malden and Oxford: Blackwell.

Yakushko, O. (2009a). Human trafficking: A review for mental health professionals. *International Journal for the Advancement of Counselling, 31,* 158–167. https://doi.org/10.1007/s10447-009-9075-3.

Yakushko, O. (2009b). Xenophobia: Understanding the roots and consequences of negative attitudes towards immigrants. *The Counseling Psychologist, 37,* 36–66.

Yakushko, O. (2010a). Stress and coping strategies in the lives of recent immigrants: A grounded theory model. *International Journal for the Advancement of Counselling, 32(4),* 256–273.

Yakushko, O. (2010b). Working through interpreters with limited-English proficiency clients: A phenomenological investigation. *Professional Psychology: Research, Theory, and Practice, 41*(5), 449–455.

Yakushko. O. (2018a). Don't worry, be happy: Erasure of racism, sexism, and poverty in positive psychology. *Psychotherapy and Politics International, 16,* e1433.

Yakushko, O. (2018b). Witches, charlatans and old-wives tales: Critical history of women's indigenous knowledge in psychology. *Women and Therapy, 41,* 18–29.

Yakushko, O. (In review). The evolution of eugenics in U.S. Psychology: On a disciplinary promotion of the "science of race betterment".

Yakushko, O., & Blodgett, E. (2018). Counseling recent immigrants. In CC. Lee (Ed.), *Multicultural issues in counseling: New approaches to diversity* (pp. 215–227). Alexandria, VA: American Counseling Association.

Yakushko, O., & Chronister, K. (2005). Immigrant women and counseling: The invisible others. *Journal of Counseling and Development, 83,* 292–299.

Yakushko, O., & Espín, O. (2010). Immigrant and refugee women. In H. Landrine & N. F. Russo (Eds.), *Handbook of diversity in feminist psychology* (pp. 535–558). Washington, DC: American Psychological Association.

Yakushko, O., & Morgan-Consoli, M. L. (2012). Immigration: Research, clinical practice and training. In N. Fouad & J. Carter (Eds.), *The handbook of counseling psychology.* Thousand Oaks: Sage.

Yakushko, O., & Morgan-Consoli, M. L. (2013). Understanding gendered adaptation: A multiple feminist case study of immigrant women. *International Journal for the Advancement of Counselling,* 36, 70–83.

Yakushko, O., & Morgan-Consoli, M. L. (2014a). Gendered stories of adaptation and resistance: A feminist multiple case study of immigrant women. *International Journal for the Advancement of Counselling, 36*(1), 70–83.

Yakushko, O., & Morgan-Consoli, M. L. (2014b). Politics and research of immigration: Implications for counseling and psychological scholarship and action. *Journal of Social Action in Counseling and Psychology, 6,* 98–122.

Yakushko, O., & Rajan, I. (2013). Refugees. In *The multicultural psychology case studies.* Thousand Oaks, CA: Sage (with student).

Yakushko, O., & Rajan, I. (2017). Global love for sale: Divergence and convergence of human trafficking with "mail order brides" and international arranged marriage phenomena. *Women & Therapy, 40*(1–2), 190–206.

Yerkes, R. M. (1923). Eugenic bearing of measurements of intelligence. *The Eugenics Review, 14*(4), 225–229.

Young, R. J. (2005). *Colonial desire: Hybridity in theory, culture and race*. New York: Routledge.
Yuval, I. J. (2011). Jews and Christians in the middle ages: Shared myths, common language. In R. S. Wistrich (Ed.), *Demonizing the other: Antisemitism, racism and xenophobia* (pp. 88–107). London, UK: Routledge.
Zinn, H. (2010). *The twentieth century: A people's history*. New York: Harper & Row.
Zizek, S. (1997). *The plague of fantasies*. London: Verso.
Zylinska, J. (2004). The universal acts: Judith Butler and the biopolitics of immigration. *Cultural Studies, 18*(4), 523–537.

Index

A
Ahmed, S., 12, 49, 78, 82, 92
Aliens, 42, 43, 46, 72, 93
 as symbol, 46
Anger, 48, 75, 93
Animals, 3, 4, 12, 16, 21, 46, 48, 62, 63, 93
 as symbol, 46
Anti-Semitism, 2, 4, 6, 12, 21, 22, 52, 63, 75, 76
 historical, 2, 21, 52
 relation to xenophobia, 4, 6, 12, 22, 52, 75
Army Mental Tests, 40
 justification for xenophobia, 52
Assimilation, 3
 relation to xenophobia, 3, 4

B
Baldwin, J., 2, 23, 37, 70
Bhabha, H., 12, 17, 22, 79, 81, 82
Biculturalism, 82
Biological explanations, 68
 support for xenophobia, 68
Bollas, C., 73, 74, 80, 81, 92
Brain abuse, 19
Brain drain, 19, 36
Brigham, C., 39–41, 47, 65

C
Cacho, L.M., 1, 2, 17, 38, 50, 71, 72, 75, 78, 79
Capitalism, 71
 relation to xenophobia, 71
Colonialism, 6, 63, 71, 72
 relation to xenophobia, 6, 63
Commodification, 47
"Conspiracy of silence", 48
Coolidge, C., 43
Criminalization, 79
Critical theories, 75, 81, 93
Cultural exchanges, 33

D
Darwin, C., 16, 21, 38, 65
Darwinism, 2, 4, 15, 17, 38, 61–63, 65, 66, 72, 91
Davenport, C., 38, 40, 41, 47
De-colonial theories, 79, 82

O. Yakushko, *Modern-Day Xenophobia*,
https://doi.org/10.1007/978-3-030-00644-0

Dehumanization of immigrants, 79
Demonization, 23, 38, 74
Diaspora, 34, 36
Discrimination, 3, 13, 18, 19, 22, 35, 51, 62, 70
Douglass, F., 44
Du Boise, W., 78

E
Education, 4, 18, 19, 43
  among immigrants, 4, 18, 19
Emotions, 49, 71, 74
  use in xenophobia, 47
Employment, 19, 44, 46
  immigrants, 19, 44, 46, 47
Environmental problems, 47
  blaming immigrants, 47
Ethnic businesses, 20
Ethnocentric Guilt, 70–73
Ethnocentrism, 6, 14, 16
  relation to xenophobia, 6, 16
Eugenics, 4, 15, 17, 38–40, 42–44, 47, 48, 62–65, 72, 91
  definition, 2, 38
  relation to xenophobia, 4, 47, 62
Evolutionary psychology, 15, 62, 65
  justifications of xenophobia, 62

F
Fanon, F., 2, 3, 17, 23, 34, 38, 70–74, 78
Fatherland, 76
  relation to xenophobia, 76
Feeble-mindedness, 39, 42
Fetishism, 12, 78, 79
  immigrants, 78, 79
Founding fiction, 79
Freud, S., 73, 75, 76, 92

G
Galton, F., 16, 21, 38, 45, 65
Gaze, 77
Gender, 3, 48, 63, 64, 67, 92, 94
  immigration, 5
Genetics, 50, 63
  justification of xenophobia, 15
Genetic Similarity Theory, 64
  justification of xenophobia, 64
Germs, 66
  justification of xenophobia, 61
Goddard, H.H., 38, 42, 48, 65

H
Hall, S., 21, 38, 39, 65, 93
Hate crime groups, 46
Heredity, 50, 82
  justification for xenophobia, 50
History, 1, 2, 4, 12, 17, 21, 22, 33–35, 37, 38, 49, 63, 70, 71, 75, 80, 93
  influence on xenophobia, 6, 23, 36
Homeland, 77
  relation to xenophobia, 77
Hostile imagination, 13
Human trafficking, 5, 38, 51, 67
Hybrid identity, 79

I
Ideology, 2, 75
  relation to xenophobia, 2
Image, 2, 68
Immigrants
  construction of the foreigner, 22, 77, 91
  racial minorities, 2, 47, 67
  refugees, 4, 34, 51
  undocumented, 4, 46, 51, 66, 75, 79

women, 3, 19, 47, 49, 78
Intelligence, 18, 38, 40–42, 47, 48, 62–66, 73
justification of xenophobia, 47, 65
Interaction with immigrants, 68, 92
Intermarriages, 33
Intersection, 4, 17
prejudices against minority groups, 4
Islamophobia, 4, 6, 22
relation to xenophobia, 6, 22

J
Just World theory, 68–70

L
Lacan, J., 77
Language, 11, 14, 16, 18, 19, 35
accented, 18
Language capacity, 18
relation to xenophobia, 18
Layton, L., 70, 71, 73, 75, 92
Lazarus, E., 6, 38, 49
Levinas, P., 77
Liberation perspectives, 94

M
Malleus Maleficarum, 2
Matriarchal and matrifocal cultures, 62
Meaning, 41, 49
Model minority, 49, 79
"Mongrel complex", 12
Motherland, 76
relation to xenophobia, 76

N
Nationalism, 14, 15
relation to xenophobia, 14
Nation-states, 1, 11, 22
Nativism, 6, 14, 15
relation to xenophobia, 6
Nazi eugenics, 39, 45, 50
relation to xenophobia, 50
Normopathic self, 80

O
Occupational downgrading, 18, 19
Oedipal theory, 76, 77
Other, 77, 78, 80
Othering, 77, 78
Overpopulation theory, 15
relation to xenophobia, 15

P
Paralogical explanations, 72
Pearson, K., 15, 16, 21, 38, 40, 45, 65
Pinker, S., 15, 62, 63, 65, 93
Pioneer Fund, 63, 64
Pleistocene era, 62, 63
mythologizing in evolutionary psychology, 62
Politics, 93
relation to xenophobia, 93
Populism, 6, 14, 15
relation to xenophobia, 14
Positive psychology, 49
support for xenophobia, 49
Post-colonial theory, 6, 22, 34, 81
Prejudice, 1–4, 11–19, 22, 23, 34, 37, 52, 61–64, 66–70, 75, 79, 82, 91–93
Prelogical explanations, 72
Procreation, 2, 15, 64, 66
Progressive, 4, 15, 23, 41, 93
xenophobia, 4, 23
Projection, 73, 77
Psychoanalytic theories, 74, 76
Psychophobia, 80, 81, 94

R
Racism, 2, 4–6, 12, 13, 16–18, 21, 33, 52, 62, 63, 70, 71, 91
  pitting immigrants against native born racial minorities, 2
  relation to xenophobia, 13, 16, 17
Realistic threat theories, 67
Relationality, 81
Religion, 22, 94
  relation to xenophobia, 22
Right-wing authoritarianism, 68, 69
Roosevelt, T., 15, 42, 43
Rushton, P., 17, 62–65

S
Said, E., 34, 82
Sanger, M., 15, 44
Sartre, J.P., 77
Self-idealization, 80
Sexism, 2, 4, 5, 47, 62, 63, 91
Skilled labor, 19
  immigrants, 19
Slavery, 17, 38, 51
  relation to xenophobia, 38
Social biology, 62
  relation to xenophobia, 62
Social Darwinism, 2, 4, 15, 17, 38, 62, 63, 65, 72, 91
Social death, 79, 92
Social Dominance Orientation, 69
Southern Poverty Law Center, 51, 63, 64
Splitting, 69, 73, 74, 77, 80, 92–94
Steele, S., 70–72
Stereotyping, 13, 51
Strangers, 11–13, 33, 36, 78, 82, 93
Symbol, 77
System Justification Theory, 69

T
Threat, 2, 13, 20, 21, 23, 36–40, 42, 44, 46, 47, 50, 66–69, 74–76, 93
  minorities as perceived threat, 67
Tide, 72
  image of immigration, 21, 33
Transgressive theories, 82
Transmissive self, 81
Trump, D., 3
  xenophobic statement, 3

U
Unconscious factors, 72, 75
The UNESCO, 91
The United Nations, 13
Universalizing prejudice, 91
Unskilled labor, 69
  immigrants, 36

V
Violence against immigrants, 3, 46

W
Wall
  as symbol, 23, 41
Wave, 1, 2
  as symbol, 2
White Guilt, 70–73
White injury, 71, 75
Witch-hunts, 4

X
Xenomania, 12
Xenophilia, 1, 12
Xenophobia

contemporary, 2, 4, 6, 12, 15, 17, 33, 34, 38, 46, 51, 63, 71, 78, 91, 93
definitions, 6, 11, 13
political statements, 1, 2

Y
Yakushko, O., 1, 2, 4, 5, 14, 15, 17–20, 23, 36, 38, 39, 46, 48–51, 62, 63, 66, 67

Z
Zinn, H., 1, 2, 22, 23, 37, 38

The manufacturer's authorised representative in the EU is Springer Nature Customer Service Centre GmbH, Europaplatz 3, 69115 Heidelberg, Germany. If you have any concerns regarding our products, please contact ProductSafety@springernature.com

Printed and bound by CPI Group (UK) Ltd, Croydon, CR0 4YY

30/09/2026

02225466-0006